Liz Hicklin's debut novel masterfully recounts this incredible true story and memoir of her sister Audrey's life and the subsequent uncovering of a bundle of letters from her long-time secret admirer. This leads to the unraveling of a most mysterious phenomenon known as Limerence, only recently attracting the attention of psychologists worldwide. Beautifully written, Limerence is a fascinating journey of obsessive love, and Hicklin manages to weave historical fact with psychological insight, exploring the limits of devotion and the true meaning of love, from behind the veil of what she exposes as a "most mysterious disease of the mind."

Susan Wakefield

Limerence

LIZ HICKLIN

Copyright 2020 by **Liz Hicklin**

Published by MMH Press
Perth, Australia

All rights reserved. No part of this book may be used or reproduced in any manner whatsoever without written permission from **Liz Hicklin**, except as provided by Australia copyright law or in the case of brief quotations embodied in articles and reviews.

The scanning, uploading and distribution of this book via the Internet or via any other means without the permission of the publisher is illegal and punishable by law.

Please purchase only authorised electronic editions and do not participate in or encourage electronic piracy of copyrighted materials. Your support of the author's rights is sincerely appreciated.

Edited by Susan Wakefield
Typeset by MMH Press

Printed in Australia
ISBN: 978-0-6487887-3-7 (sc)
ISBN: 978-0-6487887-4-4 (e)

*A state of mind that comes
from a romantic attraction
to another person.
Typically includes obsessive thoughts
and fantasies
with the object of love
and having one's feelings
reciprocated.*

*This book is dedicated to
my dear sister Audrey,
In recounting a very special part of her life.*

CONTENTS

CHAPTER ONE   11

CHAPTER TWO   16

CHAPTER THREE   28

CHAPTER FOUR   35

CHAPTER FIVE   41

CHAPTER SIX   48

CHAPTER SEVEN   55

CHAPTER EIGHT   63

CHAPTER NINE   70

CHAPTER TEN   73

CHAPTER ELEVEN   79

CHAPTER TWELVE   84

CHAPTER THIRTEEN   89

CHAPTER FOURTEEN   92

CHAPTER FIFTEEN	100
CHAPTER SIXTEEN	104
CHAPTER SEVENTEEN	107
CHAPTER EIGHTEEN	111
CHAPTER NINETEEN	114
CHAPTER TWENTY	118
CHAPTER TWENTY-ONE	133
ACKNOWLEDGEMENTS	135
ABOUT THE AUTHOR	137

CHAPTER ONE

Juliette

"I was married to a man for forty-five years who was in love with another woman."

These were my mother's angry words as we walked arm in arm from my father's funeral.

"What on earth do you mean?"

"He told me he was in love with her before we were married, I always hoped he would forget her. He went to his grave still yearning for the illusion," My mother mutters in guttural German.

"Did you ever meet her?"

"No, I think she is English. I don't know if he has seen her over the years, but she has been an ever-present ghost. I hate her. Years ago, I found a picture in his pocket of a pretty young girl, he has been clinging onto this image. She has to be old and wrinkled now."

"All those wonderful things they said about him today," Mother snarls. "I could tell them a thing or two. He was a bastard to me—not to you dear; you were his heart's darling; I was nothing but a housekeeper. You know, all those years, he never kissed me on the lips, always just a casual brush of the cheek."

I'm puzzled. Could this be my father? Someone for whom dignitaries had come from far and wide to express their admiration, a recipient of the Legion d'honneur?

We reached the big house, full of cards and flowers that had been arriving for days. Mother flung herself into an armchair and burst into tears. "I can't wait to get out of these damn funeral clothes." She tore at the buttons of her dark tailored suit and flung the little pill box hat across the room. Her greying hair, normally in a neat chignon, was now a tussle.

"Please pour me a drink, Juliette."

I busy myself with the task while struggling to come to terms with my mother's story. We had lived together in the same house for years; but they had such different tastes that Father bought this lovely villa for himself and me, furnished it with antiques, paintings and books. Mother hated these things, calling them junk, so he bought another house for her near the market and park, where she could walk her little dog.

I settle Mother with a stiff brandy and make myself comfortable on the chaise. I need to think. There is so much to take in, so many revelations. Did I really know my father? We didn't go out as a family, only to church. Dad and I holidayed together; Mother went home to her family in Germany. I am beginning to think I didn't know my father at all. I close my eyes and am beginning to doze off when I awake with a start. He had always been guarded about his desk in the study; I was never allowed to meddle with it. I wonder if there is something there, a secret?

I go to the stairs, careful not to disturb Mother. My curiosity has got the better of me. He spent hours in this room, his study. I sit at his desk and feel like an intruder. I sense his presence, I know I am the one destined to take on where my father left off.

From the window I can see the Citadel of Besçanon perched on a hill, the river Doube and the forests beyond. He was very proud of this medieval city with its beautiful historical buildings, some dating to the Middle Ages. At the foot of the hill is the Cathedral which has a unique 70 dial astronomical clock face that indicates sunset and sunrise. He would take me for walks by the river to study the clock and to see the animals parade round the structure. We would spend hours at the museum, but Mother never came with us.

Father retreated more into himself as the years went by, researching and reading reports related to the Institute, which was named in his honour. The highlight of his career was to be awarded the Legion of Honour. There were dozens of people from his academic circles filling the pews this morning, all full of admiration for this great man. This room, his den, with its book-lined shelves, looks out onto the meadows, with the views of the mountains in the distance. I look over the dozens of leather-bound law books that I coveted when I was studying.

He loved the French writers, Flaubert's Madam Bovary—Father wouldn't let me read that one until I went to college, but when I finally did I didn't know what all the fuss had been about. The Count of Monte Cristo—Victor Hugo—came from Besçanon. He loved his music, Bach's Air on a G string; he said it soothed one's soul.

I kick off my high heels, take off my couture jacket and loosen my blouse as I delve further into father's life. Tears are blinding me now. I feel his presence as I sit at his desk. It's a mass of papers, and I don't know where to start. This desk must be hundreds of years old. There are compartments at the back, all sorts of hidey-holes, even a drawer with a silver knob. I gently pull on it. Letters wrapped in a bundle, tied with faded pink satin ribbon spill out. What on earth have I stumbled on here? I suddenly feel guilty. This is my father's life. I feel like an intruder but...

I delve further. The letters are old aerograms, faded blue thin tissue-like paper, addressed to Hubert Bisset, written in English, dated 1949. Could these be special, maybe even love letters? I remember Father telling me that he went to England to work as a volunteer for the Olympic Games in 1948. He used to say it was the most exciting time of his life. There is a battered little note book which looks as though it has been well thumbed through, and a note on the front of it written in Father's cursive handwriting.

'If ever I should die please send these to Audrey. Everything I have written is for her. She has been my grand adventure from which I am still suffering. She has been my only friend and I will keep forever my eternal devotion to this beautiful woman.'

My hands are shaking, my face streaked with tears. 'My eternal devotion.' What beautiful words from my father's soul. Such love. Such devotion.

I can picture him now, sitting in his favourite chair, arms pinned behind his head nodding self-assuredly at his well-kept secret. He is watching me, silent in the knowledge that now is the time for his secrets to be unearthed. He liked me to know things. "Law," he would say, "Follow the law."

I drink in my father's life, making it mine. My eyes are shining, my heart aflame.

"Juliette," mother calls. "Where are you?"

I quickly bundle the letters and the book back into the desk and close the lid. It is unbelievable; the dreams, the secrets my father had all those years.

I shan't tell Mother of my discovery; it would be too painful. This funeral day has been long enough already for her to bear, and her nerves are shot to pieces.

CHAPTER TWO

Audrey

The 1948 Olympic Games are happening in London in July, and they are calling for volunteers. I have been accepted and will be on holiday from my teacher training course. We will be billeted in Nissen Huts in a disused R.A.F. camp. There has been so much controversy about holding the Games so soon after the war, Europe still being in a state of austerity, with clothes and food rationing, displaced people and bombed-out cities. The powers that be have decided that it was better for men to jump and run against each other, rather than blow each other to pieces on the battlefield.

Wembley Stadium has been chosen as the venue, after having spent thousands of pounds converting it from a greyhound racing

Limerence

track. Other nations have chipped in and helped. Some, like Sweden and Finland have donated the wood to replace the rotting seats. Television has been invented, and no doubt sales of tickets will be boosted. I don't think my father will be tempted to purchase a television set; he probably thinks it is wicked.

The officials are adamant that all contestants be amateur and have not previously earned money from their sport. The British contestants have been trained at Butlins' Holiday Camp, which has a private beach and swimming pool. Teams from New Zealand and Australia have been at sea for six weeks, doing what training they could on rough seas. The Americans sailed in style across the Atlantic, black and white athletes mingling together.

Many of the athletes have been billeted with locals and will be introduced to different cuisine and customs. London is swarming with athletes, coaches and visitors from all over the world; many are obviously disturbed by the bomb-damaged buildings and vacant lots. Visitors are impressed by the kindness of the English who generally show their appreciation for war-time food parcels. Not all people are happy about the Games being held, as they are still suffering austerity.

Nevertheless, the Olympic Torch was lit by the rays of the sun at the Temple of Zeus and sped by a succession of runners through Europe, being diverted through Pierre de Colubrine, to avoid having to run through Germany.

I am lucky, having already bought a ticket for the Opening Ceremony tomorrow, although the forecast is for a very hot day. Athletes wearing their blazers have been seen getting preferential treatment in restaurants, their plates piled high. I will be working in the Hungarian restaurant, lots of potatoes and goulash. Some teams have even brought their own food and chefs, and the French large quantities of wine! Down the road, the Australian Cricket team, captained by Don Bradman, are beating England yet again—they have played thirty matches without losing one!

I have joined the thousands down Olympic Way. On the radio they said it is the hottest day since 1911–ninety-three degrees. It is sweltering. I find my reserved seat eventually, tripping over men with folded newspapers and knotted handkerchiefs over their heads. Women have rolled down their silk stockings and are using their umbrellas as parasols.

Despite the temperature, the band of the Massed Guards marches around in their red woollen jackets and bearskin hats. The Union Jack and the Olympic flag fly on the twin towers of the stadium, while all around flutter the flags of the competing nations. The stands are like gigantic hanging gardens of flowers, blue and pink. I feel very proud of my country, patriotism pumping through my veins.

I become aware of a man sitting beside me. I remark that the seats are hard, and before I know it he has hired a cushion and placed it underneath me. What a gallant gentleman, I think.

I turn to look at him, tall and handsome with flashing brown eyes, olive skin and a sharp nose. He is wearing an open neck shirt and fawn slacks. Mmmm, yes, very attractive. I look more closely, taking in his stature, noting that he has the habit of flicking his brown hair away from his forehead. He doesn't look English. Sure enough, he speaks with a French accent.

"Bonjour, I am Hubert," he says softly, in my direction.

"Bonjour," I manage to say, in my English accented French.

"Ca Va?" He replies again quickly. I return a puzzled look, confused.

Limerence

"Oh, pardon, mademoiselle; I assume that you can speak the French way but you do not. This is okay, I will speak English for you." He gestures and an easy friendliness arrives between us.

"I'm Audrey," I reply. I have never met a Frenchman before, and find his accent quite seductive. We have a good view of the Royal box, which is overflowing with dignitaries dressed in coloured robes. Everyone cheers when the Royal family takes their place, especially when Princess Margaret arrives, having recently recovered from measles. The Frenchman roars when I tell him these little tidbits. I explain that the King, George the Sixth, is not very robust. He is fifty-one years old now and does look thin and weak, although he walks erect, in full uniform. I just hope there is an electric fan in the royal box.

Hubert is fascinated, the French haven't had royalty for years. Several men in top hat and tails, a carnation in their buttonholes swelter in the heat; what a price to pay for being an aristocrat.

At three o'clock the Grenadier Guards strike up the 'March of Gladiators, 'and the athletes begin to file in. The Greek team lead first because they were the originators of the Olympics, then the rest in alphabetical order. I wave my flag and cheer like mad as the one lone Maltese athlete marches by; that little island got such a pounding in the war and it has hardly recovered.

I'm aware of the Frenchman looking at me intently and I feel a bit embarrassed, noting that continental men are different – or so I have been told.

The French team marching by divert his attention. The U. S. Women's team look the smartest, in white pleated skirts and elegant high heels. I wonder how they are feeling, marching in this heat. The British team had to use their own clothing coupons for white cotton frocks and a blue blazer with the Union Jack on the pocket.

I cheer madly when the British team march by, and nearly fall off the stand. Hubert catches me, and for a moment hangs on to me. Oh my, I feel embarrassed.

The whole parade is a sea of colour, men and women cheering, chanting, waving flags, so emotional after six hard years of war. I am so thrilled to be here.

At four o'clock the King announces, "Let the Games Begin." Trumpeters in glorious red and gold uniforms and white breeches sound a fanfare. Above the stadium, we watch spellbound as the white Olympic flag with five Olympic rings, signifying five continents, breaks open in the breeze. The next moment we are engulfed in pigeons, three hundred and fifty baskets of racing pigeons having arrived that morning from all over Europe, and are duly released at four o'clock.

The flash of wings is like a snow storm surrounding us. I grab Hubert without thinking; we look at each other and burst out laughing. As I stare at the birds the world suddenly falls silent, just for a moment. The birds encircle the stadium three times, the Royal artillery fires a 21-gun salute and the pigeons scatter.

Then, a magnificent specimen of manhood comes roaring down the track bearing the Olympic Torch. He circles the stadium, his chest proudly inflated. He runs right past us, up the ramp and lights the flame above his head. Everybody is going crazy and I unconsciously grab hold of Hubert's sleeve again, stirred by the emotion of it all. Music, edifying and patriotic rings out across the stadium. Sir Malcom Sergeant is conducting the London Philharmonic Orchestra and a massed choral society sings Rudyard Kipling's 'Not unto us O' Lord.'

I feel goosebumps and am so proud to be British. The choir sings Handel's Hallelujah chorus and the captain of the British team declares the Games open. The flag bearers march out, followed by the teams. I sigh, sitting next to the French boy and we continue like that for many minutes, stunned by the majesty of it all. He breaks our shared silence and I realise that all this time I have had my fingers wrapped around his sleeve. I blush again. We discover we are billeted in the same R.A.F camp, so we battle through the crowd and get home just in time for me to don my uniform and serve dinner in the Hungarian tent. Huge men eat goulash, fisherman's soup, chicken paprika and stuffed cabbage rolls.

The French boy seems pretty keen, persistent as well. I am seeing him again tonight. We're going to the film,' Annie Get Your Gun.'

***

Hubert goes back to his digs with only one thing on his mind, this stunning English girl, so beautiful, he can hardly believe his luck. A flawless complexion and such pretty gold locks tamed in a bob. Perfect figure, what a knockout she is; and such a gorgeous smile, beautifully decked out in a flowery summer dress. When she smiles her whole face lights up, so much more attractive than the stuck-up French girls back home. He rushes through his chores cleaning the athlete's quarters. He wants to make a good impression, so he arrives at her door promptly with a bunch of flowers. She gives him the loveliest smile, then looks a bit embarrassed, saying it is the first time a man has given her flowers. She pops them back in her room, watched by the curious girls who share her Nissen Hut.

Hubert can't concentrate on the film, and wants to put his arm around Audrey, hold her hand, but resists, not wanting her to think him forward. The English are more reserved, he's been told, but her very presence beside him is electrifying.

***

We walk home through Hyde Park on a beautiful balmy night, it is still quite light. Hubert suggests we rest, puts his jacket on the grass, and we lie down by the Serpentine.

"Tell me about your life in England during the war?" he asks. "You weren't invaded, but I know you were bombed mercilessly."

"I was just eleven years old when war was declared, and like most English children, I was evacuated to the country. I remember my mother tearfully sewing name tags on my sister's and my liberty bodices. I told Mother not to be upset, that it would soon be over, but I was secretly looking forward to a new adventure. We were all given a carry-bag containing a tin of bully beef, a tin of condensed milk and the largest block of chocolate I had ever seen. Our parents waved nervously— no one knew what the future held.

We travelled by train to a village not far from Manchester, and with another pair of sisters were told that we were to be billeted at the Doctor's house. We were instructed to walk up the street as far as the Maypole, it was the house with the wrought iron fence. We found this rather grand forbidding house and walked up the winding path. I was the tallest, so I stood on tip-toe and banged on the big brass knocker. A dog's bark greeted us, nothing else mattered; they had a dog. A young girl in a maid's uniform opened the door, and a black cocker spaniel jumped around excitedly. The other sisters had clung together nervously. "Come in," the maid had said, "We have been waiting for you."

Limerence

We were led into a large kitchen and sat down to a meal of bread and plum jam. This was to be our staple meal every tea time. A grey haired lady introduced herself, saying her name was Miss Auburn, and the maid was called Bretta.

Annie the cook, another older lady dressed in a long blue dress and white apron, stood in front a huge black stove, her grey hair tied in a bun. She looked flustered like Mother on a baking day, worrying about all the extra mouths she had to feed.

An older man popped his head in. Miss Auburn introduced him as "Dr. Auburn, my brother," adding "We have agreed to take you in as our contribution to the war effort."

Then a cheery man, in a blue uniform, waved at us from an open door. "This is John the chauffeur," said Miss Auburn, then added, "Shot, settle down," pointing to the dog under the table. He could have licked me forever.

After tea Miss Auburn asked Bretta to show us to our bedroom. We climbed the wide carpeted stairs and were shown into a room with two brass beds, a wardrobe and a washstand containing a jug and basin which Bretta filled every morning with warm water for us to wash. Miss Auburn supervised our bathing every night at six-thirty in six inches of water as decreed by the King.

Life was regimented; the other two sisters were unhappy and moved away to a small cottage. Our clothes were laid out every morning, black woollen stockings for week-days and brown ones on Sundays. We ate at the big kitchen table with our own individual steam puddings drizzling with hot jam and custard. Sunday lunch was shared with the Doctor and Miss Auburn in a beautiful dining room with fine china and silver tureens, and this was where I learned to use finger bowls. One night there was a bad air raid and the doctor invited the owners of the fairground carnival to share our basement air-raid shelter. I was more terrified by the black-eyed gypsies than the bombers pounding industrial Manchester.

Our father was a Methodist lay preacher, he would call by if he was preaching in the area, always with flowers for Miss Auburn and new dresses for us. He left strict rules that we were not allowed to go to the cinema on Saturday afternoons with the rest of the village children and there was to be strict attendance at Sunday school.

Each week I would walk through the fog and blackout to my music lesson with Mr Harrow. I wore a white pixie hood and an illuminated button because of the blackout. One day Mr Harrow rested his hand on my knee, I had the feeling that it wasn't right but I had no one to tell.

"Hubert," I say, looking solemnly at him, "I have never told anyone all of this."

Hubert lies down next to her; he is transfixed, and does not what to say. He feels light headed;, butterflies are everywhere inside him. So entranced is he, he can't get enough of her.

"How different were my war experiences," he manages to say. "Maybe I will tell you sometime."

"Yes, I would like to hear them." I say. "I was neither a village kid nor a member of the aristocracy. One day a friend was visiting Miss Auburn, Lady something or other, bringing her daughter who was my age. I heard her discussing with her brother whether I, being an evacuee, should be allowed to play with the daughter of a lady. The class system is alive and well in Britain— is it the same in France?"

"France is very snobby really, my father wants me to be a lawyer—he would die if I said I was going to be a plumber." We both laugh at that.

"The war ended and no one wanted to be servants anymore. Bretta had joined the services. Dr Auburn died, Annie retired and Miss Auburn was unable to find a housekeeper. Poor lady, she had been brought up as a lady and could not fend for herself. She moved into a smaller house with only Shot the dog. I went back to Manchester, to High School which I loved, especially sport and art. I always wanted to be a teacher, so now I am at a training college and hope one day to teach 'The History of Art.'"

"Oh, you must come to Paris to the Louvre—we have the finest art of anywhere in the world. A lot of it was hidden from the Germans but it is being re-installed in the Louvre and Musee d'Orsay. The French impressionists and the modern artists, Picasso and the Surrealists. Paris is a beautiful city; I'd love to show you around," he tells me excitedly.

"I would love to come, maybe next holiday. Once I start earning money as a teacher, I will be free to do whatever I like."

We walk home in the twilight, hand in hand. He gives me a light kiss and tells me that he wants to see me every day that we are here.

"I want you to show me Westminster Abbey, Houses of Parliament, Changing of the Guard and see as much of the Games as we can."

It is a whirlwind of a time, and the scorching heat is followed by torrential rain. We are lucky to see the Hungarian Zatopek in the marathon, enter the stadium drenched in mud, every step the biggest effort of his life, losing only by two one-hundredths of a second to Reif. The crowd goes wild cheering him on. Another highlight we see is the Dutch Hurdler, Fanny Blinkers-Koen, a thirty year old mother of two, win her race.

It all comes to an end with the Closing Ceremony, which is pretty low-key. Hubert says he feels the end of his time with me is looming. Many of the athletes have left for home, but the few remaining march around sporting their medals. The King and Queen have already left for Balmoral, but there are still a few dignitaries in the Royal box to salute. At six o'clock, the Olympic flag is handed to the Mayor of London and the flame is extinguished. The Games are over.

Our final night together. Gunfire is followed by fireworks that light the night sky, the likes of which we haven't seen since the V for Victory night. There is an air of wild abandonment, the games have brought world peace after the horrors of war. There is an overwhelming sense of positivity and good will that the Games have brought to players and spectators alike. It feels like a new beginning. We watch as countries dance and mingle, the big band plays and trumpets scream forth, signalling victory and heralding this Olympic Games as the most momentous Games ever.

Hubert takes pictures of me with his box brownie; even in my waitresses 'uniform. He says I have a perfect figure and look like a movie star.

It is a night of endless partying, but all Hubert can see is the girl with the magnificent sparkle in her eyes. He feels so lucky to be with her and as proud as a peacock sporting her on his arm—he cannot stop thinking what a great girl she is, and the unforgettable stories shared, the closeness felt, the undeniable connection.

We reach the Athletes' village; me to the dining room, him to clean the apartments. He watches me walk away with all the poise and presence I can muster.

We exchange telephone numbers and addresses; he pleads for just one more meeting in the morning before his Channel crossing. I agree, commenting on the persistence of Frenchmen. We meet again briefly to say our final goodbyes. Hubert looks an emotional wreck. He gives me one white rose, telling me he has never been so happy in his entire life.

I'm touched and I see tears well in his eyes. We kiss longingly, meaningfully; it's been nice, this little romance, but I must return to teacher's college and Hubert to his studies. We resolve to write every week and meet next holidays, and slowly, reluctantly comes the untwining of fingers, and we part.

CHAPTER THREE

Hubert

I board the channel crossing; it is even rougher than the last time, and I am lost in grief at having to leave the girl who has completely stolen my heart. At home everybody is anxious to hear about the Games and London. I tell them my adventures, but not about Audrey; they'd call me stupid.

But I do tell my best friend Jacques about meeting my English rose, of our great time together; he is green with envy, then rolls his eyes and tries to change the subject. I show him my photos, and he is quick to agree that she is a stunner.

"Yes, she is a beautiful English girl, Hubert, as fine as a dainty English china teacup. Look at that perfect porcelain skin, rosy lips and painted nails...but you hardly know her. How old? Nineteen? Too perfect. And English as well." He snorts at my stupidity.

Limerence

"Oh, but Jacques my friend, just wait until you meet her!"

"Are you going to see her again?"

"Yes, I hope so. We agreed we would write to each other until we can find a suitable time between her studies and mine, but seriously, Jacques, I don't think I can wait that long!"

My father wants me to go to Law school, but I am not so sure. He doesn't want me to work on the paper with him, thinks I'm better suited to law. I can't enthuse about anything. Our town is so dull after London. I write to Audrey every week and wait patiently for the post, feeling miserable if he doesn't leave me a letter. I think of her constantly, her lovely silk hair and shapely figure. As I grabbed her and held her close for one final kiss I knew that she was The One. That's not wrong, is it? I wonder if she feels the same about me? Or am I just a romantic Frenchman caught in the excitement of the Games?

Jacques interrupts my thoughts.

"You and I, Hubert—we are passionate French men; it is in our blood, we cannot help it," Jacques shrugs. "But this girl is English, and we are better to stay with our own—"

I do not let him finish, I will not hear it. We part, and I go home to think about my new love. She is the pinnacle of my existence; I can think of nothing else and can't get her out of my mind. I am a love-sick train wreck.

The only thing that calms me is to write to her. I sit at my desk, find my writing pad and begin.

"Dearest Audrey..." my heart starts racing. I don't know what to say. I sigh and put down the pen. Already my life feels boring without her.

The hot August nights turn to crisp September days and the heat of the summer slowly disappears, replaced by the crisp winds of Autumn. The leaves begin to fall. I think of Audrey day and night. I wonder what she is doing, is she happy, is she alone, is she lonely, does she think of me at all? In my mind I am still dancing with her, butterflies invade my entire being, and the way she looked at me that night fills me still with hope and fervour. I sit and gather my thoughts.

I put one of the photos in a frame by my bed. She is the last thing I see at night, and the first thing I lay eyes on each morning. There's a special photo I keep in my wallet, looking at it a dozen times a day. My mother heartily agrees that Audrey is a stunner, but thinks I am too young to get serious about anyone. I quietly disagree with her, and keep the secrets, the longings, the vigilant prayers to myself. Dear Jesus, I say, let me soon be reunited with this girl. I am totally in love with her.

I buy a dozen aerograms, put on some music, and sit down to pen the next letter. I am almost sick everyday waiting for the post and watch intently from my window, pining for her, lovesick as I am. When he stops, I tear downstairs to grab the mail before anyone else; if there is a letter from England I run upstairs to my room, hurriedly close the door, lie on my bed and relish every word she has written. I think my English is improving, in both reading and writing. She has such distinctive handwriting; her letters are like her personality, bright and breezy. I find some pink ribbon in mother's sewing box, and use it to tie them together and hide them in my top drawer. Sometimes at night I take them out and read them all over again; I study each word with fascination. Like her, they are perfect and beautifully written. How could such a lovely creature ever exist, I wonder? I imagine her delicate hands holding the pen, her long, perfectly manicured nails as she elegantly scribes each word ever so gently, precisely, without wobbles, misspellings or errors. She is just perfection.

Jacques wants me to go hiking for a few days, as we usually go up to the mountains every summer, take a tent, fish in a stream. The Alps attracts hikers, fishermen, campers and skiers year-round. The scenery is a stunning winter backdrop, with postcard picture views in every direction as far as the eye can see. Other years I have been eager to go, but this year I want to be here when the letters arrive. I don't tell him, just make lame excuses about the weather. He is getting quite cross and talks about going with his brother. I just don't care anymore.

Besçanon, October 1949

Dearest Audrey,
The sun is shining as it was not so long ago in London upon your radiant skin. I still carry you in my heart, you are once again in my arms and we are dancing the night away without a care in the world. The Games are over, but my heart is with you.
Forever Yours,
Hubert

Audrey returns a short note saying that she is busy with her teaching studies, and other commitments. I immediately pen another response and run down the hill to the mailbox. I tell her how I miss her; I hope she is doing well and that she is always in my thoughts.

I cannot escape these feelings; it is both unadulterated romance and torture that I cannot shake. I think about writing another letter despite the fact that she has not responded to the last one. I know that she has had a holiday in Switzerland and I begin to wonder why she did not come here. I know I have to keep the connection going; perhaps she has been too busy with her studies to write. Even as the shorter October nights come I am consumed by Audrey, spending hours dreaming and fantasising.

My parent's concern for me has reached new heights; I have no appetite, and mope around like a bear with a sore head. The letters used to come every couple of weeks but it has been a month now and nothing has arrived. I am frantic with worry.

I know Audrey has a long summer holiday and is expecting to start teaching near her home in Manchester. I am supposed to start my university course to become a lawyer but have no heart for it. I wonder if she has had an accident; my heart flutters in panic at the thought. I put pen to paper trying to be bright, breezy and nonchalant. It is now two months without a word and all I can do is mope about the house, barely able to dress myself. I am analysing every word of every letter; scrutinising every sentence, things in my mind playing and jumping around, forming new plot disasters, reasons why she has not written? I torture myself but I know there is no way out; this is my private dance between the heartstrings of worry and desire, my fantasies taking me on all uncertain routes. I am the sole passenger on a train waiting desperately for it to stop, not knowing what station or where to get off. I continue to write to Audrey although no news is forthcoming. On a chilly April morning I awake to glistening sun breaking through the curtains of my bedroom window. I pull myself up, dress in my warmest clothes, and make my morning café au lait. I put on my long winter coat and make my way to the mailbox.

There it sits, the letter, I recognise the hand writing instantly.

Limerence

N. Manchester April 28th, 1949

Dear Hubert,

I have just returned from my holiday in Switzerland to receive your second letter from Lille. Please don't think that I have neglected you by not writing sooner. An escapist by nature, I tend to put things off as far as possible—and besides, I haven't quite known what to say. The problem of how to deal with the situation is rather perplexing.

You see Hubert, in order to steer such spiritual things as one's emotions into definite channels is sheer futility. I wish I had the wisdom of Solomon— as I haven't, I'll have to use all the tact I can muster.

Hubert, I am afraid you've got it all wrong and I'll tell you right now that my motives for marriage are definitely not those that you mentioned. I happen to love the object of my affections. However, that's irrelevant, I just wonder whether you possess sentiment—or sentimentality—when you callously suggest I should marry, with other motives in mind.

You see, Hubert, although you might have feelings for me, I never thought of our liaison as other than a friendship. I enjoyed meeting you, but I have met this Swiss boy and my motives for marriage are pure. I wonder if you are going to be ok when I write to you so bluntly as this. Unfortunately, we live in a civilisation that forces us to hurt people sometimes—mindfully or otherwise.

Dear Hubert, I am sorry it has to be this way, but my mind is made up. Nothing that you say can deter me. I wonder if you are hurt by me telling you this, and I am sorry it has to be this way— by that I mean I regret you having poured out your emotions into *such an undeserving channel as myself —it is useless to dwell on what might have been, but who can blame me for following my heart?*

Moreover, after the rush of your emotions I can't help speculating on what your conclusion would be—you would realise that there is nothing exceptional at all about me. Life is short—and by this time I am willing to bet you have dismissed the whole thing completely. Honesty after all, that is the best policy.

I am saying goodbye, let me wish you good luck and plenty of happiness in the future.

Yours,
Audrey.

CHAPTER FOUR

Hubert

I simply cannot accept that letter from Audrey. A *Swiss* of all people! My life is over, I am going to shoot myself. They didn't suffer in the war like we did. She must have met a Swiss man at some sort of conference and they have had a romance. I am shattered, I refuse to believe it, the letter tells me that she has decided to marry him. "No Audrey, no— you can't do this! You are in love with me! You can't possibly think of another." I am shattered, I fall on my knees on the wet earth looking for reasons to live. I am broken, inconsolable and weep like a baby. I should have known, at least suspected something. I hadn't heard from her for such a long time, and I refuse to believe it could be this. I wonder where she met him? I hate the Swiss, they are so goddamn boring and particular with their neat little green fields, the cleanest cows you have ever seen with their stupid clanging bells. I bet he is rich too. No, no, no! Merde! Shit! I shout to the sky above. All the hope is drained from my face, gone out of my life. I can't eat, I can't sleep. I am bitter, and drink the vermouth, absinthe and whisky at once, anything I can get my hands on. I have no desire to study the law or anything else. I have nothing to live for.

I might convince her to change her mind if I could go to see her. I am not going to study law now, I don't care what my father says. I plead with him to pay for another channel crossing. I must change her mind. Eventually, he gives in, but only if I promise to toe the line when I return home. I give him my word that I will go back to study when I have resolved things with Audrey. He shakes his head, thinks I am ridiculous, calls me a "fou-fou," a crazy person, then goes and smokes his pipe.

The next day I race to catch the train to the ferry. I cannot miss it. The weather is rough this time of year, and the seas are high; we might as well be in a dingy the way we are tossed about in huge swells, but I focus on practising my English. I travel from Folkestone to London by train and change to the Manchester line. It is a very long trip and I am exhausted when I arrive. It is late in the evening, but the blood rushes through my veins when I realise that we are under the same patch of sky. I wonder what she is doing; she has no idea I am coming, but I will find her and get her to change her mind, my sweet English rose.

I don't have enough money for hotels, so I sleep at the station on a bench. I wake feeling awful, so I ask for directions and find the YMCA. Even though this poor city got a pelting in the war, the people are friendly and helpful; I just hope Audrey is the same. I have a swim at the club followed by a hot shower to freshen up and look my best for Audrey. My eyes look tired from lack of sleep, and I find a place to eat.

Audrey will be teaching all day, so I will fill in time by wandering round the streets and catch her on the way home. To think that we are in the same town! I have goose bumps at the thought of seeing her again, it makes me half sick. My fixation with this woman has me in a vice which will not be released until she is mine. I come across the Manchester Art Gallery; it is quite an imposing building and is a good place to pass time. I wander past the statues and into the picture gallery, recognising the great masters. Not bad for a provincial city I think, not a patch on the Louvre of course, one would not expect it.

I am impressed by a local artist, L. S. Lowry. His pictures depict everyday life in this industrial city, chimneys belching thick smoke and the city shrouded in fog. Life here must be pretty miserable in winter. I must get Audrey out of this terrible place to my town of Besçanon with its clear skies and green meadows, it is a much healthier place to live.

I catch the trolley bus to her suburb; what a long monotonous road it is, rows of little shops and a public house on every corner. I arrive at Audrey's school and watch spellbound as children begin to pour out. I comb my hair, straighten my tie. I'm waiting, waiting.

I hope I have the right school. All the children seem to have left, now only the occasional adult trickles out. Then I catch sight of her talking to one of the girls, probably discussing homework. She is wearing a cream blouse and a smart check skirt, and looks so fresh and beautiful, as gorgeous as ever, clutching her papers, hair flying in the breeze. I don't want to frighten her. She catches sight of me, looks puzzled, then recognises me. I am sure she can't believe it.

"Hello, Hubert. What on earth are you doing here?"

"I came to see you, just you," I say, and kick at invisible dirt with my shoe. "We need to talk. I got your letter, but cannot possibly accept what you say. Listen, I have to go into the French army for my national service soon, then I will study law. Please, Audrey, we are meant for each other."

She looks around, visibly uncomfortable with what I have just said, and fiddles with her sleeve.

"Well, Hubert, this just isn't a suitable place to talk. There's a park just over the road. Let's go there."

I want to take her hand, but do not dare. We come to a little park and sit on a bench. She puts her papers down beside her, saying she had a lot of correcting to do as it is exam time.

"Do you like your job?" I ask.

"Yes, I actually love it. I really wanted to be an actress, so this is the next best thing - performing in front of a class of girls every day. I was a bit upset at what the head mistress said to me today."

I listen intently, I just love to hear her talking, and hang on every word.

"My girls are fifteen years old and can leave school whenever they want, but I was told today that I shouldn't worry if they are not performing well, because when they leave school they will just be factory fodder. I was so very angry. I walked away, saying under my breath, 'not if I have anything to do with it. 'As you see, Manchester is very industrial, but there *is* life beyond. I am determined to broaden their horizons. We have been on bus trips to stately homes some miles from here in the beautiful countryside. We take a picnic, I arrange a treasure hunt among the statues, they love it, some have never been outside the city. I make it my business to encourage them to venture to the outside world. There is more to life than Manchester City and United football teams."

The words of T. S. Eliot come into my mind:

"Lost in the dark caverns of her throat, bruised by the ripple of unseen muscle."

That's me. Lovelorn.

Then I notice the ring: I feel sick.

"Audrey, I am here to try and make you change your mind. I just had to talk to you."

She laughs, she actually laughs out loud.

"Hubert, you have got it all wrong, it was only ever a light romance between us. I am sorry you have come all this way. I am serious about my Swiss fiancé , the wedding is arranged and everything. I am sorry I can't ask you home, my parents would think it improper as I am engaged. Sorry, I think I should go; I have a lot of marking to do tonight."

That beautiful ring flashes at me. I feel sick again.

"So, you never felt as I did?" I ask, deflated.

"I can't relate to your feelings; we did have a happy time together but I never considered it more than a harmless flirtation."

Oh God, if only she knew. I pull my jacket tight around me. Suddenly I feel very cold.

"Look Audrey, I can't offer you much now, but when I am a successful lawyer you will have the most handsome villa in town. We will have happy children and holiday wherever your heart desires. France is a beautiful country; our cuisine is the best in the world. Audrey, you have to believe me." I notice that she is beginning to look bored, so I decide to back off.

"Look Hubert, please don't go any further, I am engaged to someone else. I am mortified that you came all this way to such an undeserving person as me." She takes a deep breath, and stands.

"Goodbye Hubert. I am sure you will forget me in no time." She starts to walk away.

My heart feels like lead. "Au revoir, mon Amie," I mumble, and walked out of her life, tears stinging my eyes.

Limerence

CHAPTER FIVE

Hubert

My call up papers and order to join the French Army of occupation in Germany come as a bit of a relief. It solves my parent's problem of what to do with their son moping around all day, unable to shake off the intense fever of 'Audrey. 'My trip to England didn't change her mind, and I have never felt such despair as I watched her walk away. I know in my heart that it is not the end. Isn't there a song, 'Yet I love her till I die? 'I'm so bereft that I know I will not study law and do not care what father says. I have nothing to live for now.

My father used to say when we were occupied by the Germans, "I will not give in," but now I feel that my life cannot go on. Oh God, I cannot live without my Audrey—but something happens to divert me. I receive a letter saying I have to report to the army camp the following day. It is so different, so unlike anything I have even known, but there is no escape. They shave my head, give me stiff rough clothes. The training is brutal—I am not used to all this physical exercise. I lose a few kilos, my muscles get used to it, and I make a few friends. The sergeant is a bully, but I suppose that is his job. He inspects the barracks every morning before we go on patrol; I pity anyone who hasn't got their gear spick and span.

At least I am learning a bit of discipline, which will please Father. The three powers, America, Russia and the U. K. have divided up Germany, and France had been given the South East along the Swiss border. This was done at England's behest in honour of the enormous contribution we made to the defeat of the Third Reich. The area I am sent to is a town near near Freiburg, lots of forests and farming, not so much touched by the war. I have been put on patrol, supposedly to guard a crossroads through which escaping Nazis might go, but the only people I see are displaced Germans trying to get to the east. I stand, trying to look stern with my rifle by my side, marching around and dreaming. Thinking of her, my Audrey, my sweetheart.

A timber worker stares at me, walks away, shrugging. I stand under a tree, bored. I eat my rations, some kind of sausage again, start to doze, but sense movement down the hill towards the village. I look up and see a young girl walking towards me. I wonder what she is up to; so far only the farm workers have walked past. She is a pretty thing wearing a flowery summer dress, her blonde plaits wrapped around her head in typical German fashion with the fresh open face of a farm girl. She smiles as she gets near.

"Bonjour, Monsieur, comment allez-vous?" I nod, she is trying very hard to speak French despite her thick German tongue.

What on earth is she up to? We aren't supposed to fraternise. I reply in my school boy German.

"Guten tag Fräulein."

"Monsieur—" she is struggling to speak, then in a mix of French and German says," I am eighteen years old, one of five sisters; not one man has returned from the war to our village."

I pick up enough to know what she means.

She looks down sheepishly, picks a blade of grass before continuing.

" I would like to be married. Please, will you marry me?"

I cannot believe my ears. A complete stranger is wanting to marry me? What do I say, what do I do?

"What is your name?" I ask.

"Heidi." She says softly, earnestly.

Now I have to use the same kind of mixed language.

"Give me time to think." After a minute or two I tell her my decision.

"Heidi, come and see me tomorrow. My name is Hubert."

She bids me au revoir, and skips off down the meadow. I watch her go, my head spinning. What on earth do I do? I go back to the barracks in turmoil. Images of Audrey's sweet face return to me again and again during the night, but by morning I think perhaps it will help me to get Audrey out of my mind.

Heidi is quite a pretty girl, probably a farm girl, she would make a good wife. What would my parents think—their son, married to a German when we have hated them for years? I daren't tell any of the boys in the barracks, they will think I have lost my mind. A German wife, after all we have been through? My family would never accept it. I think about the war and how France has suffered. Memories come flooding back.

I am ten years old and can hear the sound of the jackboots outside my window. I hate the German soldiers, even though they occasionally try to be friendly, kicking a soccer ball round the oval, but I always walk away. School is chaotic, most of the teachers having gone to war. Mr Rubenstein, my favourite teacher, is made to wear a star on his jacket; then he disappears and all the other Jews in town as well. It is only now that we are learning what happened to them, so how could I possibly bring myself to marry a German? Hordes of refugees swarmed through our village, pushing carts piled with their pitiful belongings.

My mother, a doctor at the local hospital, worked from dawn to dusk tending the sick with very few supplies. When the medicines arrived, the German officers demanded that she hand over the morphine and other drugs for their use; she had none left for her patients.

My father, editor of the Lille newspaper, was forced to print propaganda for them. Father played a big part in the French Resistance; they met in our cellar talking in hushed tones, someone was always on the look-out. Anti-aircraft fire rattled away all night, their beams criss-crossing the night skies. Sometimes local farmers would bring in a wounded British airman who had bailed out of a damaged plane, his parachute caught in a tree. They would stay in our cellar and my mother and I would take down food until arrangements were made for them to move on. They were always so polite and grateful. I would practise my English on them and used to wonder if they made it home.

My father printed pamphlets which I left on park benches when no one was around. They encouraged local factory workers to sabotage the explosives that they were making for the Germans by filling them with sawdust. My mother didn't know about this; if the enemy had found out we would have been shot.

Once the Allied troops had landed, the Germans were in full retreat, and a bedraggled pathetic bunch of prisoners tramped through our village begging for food. Everyone was starving. The English had said, 'Let the Germans starve', but everyone wanted their revenge. There is still a shortage of food in Europe, but now, at least as a soldier, I get my daily rations.

I am standing in the same spot at the edge of the village; today is not as boring as it has been. If the Sergeant Major knew, I doubt he would have sent me on patrol here today. I can see a girl coming up the meadow carrying some flowers. It is she again; yes, I see she is quite pretty, but not as beautiful as Audrey.

She hands me the flowers; I am not sure what to do with them. I hide them in the sentry box. She smiles but says nothing, so I say, "Heidi, I am in love with another girl whom I cannot marry, but if you are happy with that, then yes, I will marry you." I watch as a broad smile takes over her face; she's almost jumping for joy.

"I like cooking and am good at it, and I love babies," she says, smiling uncontrollably. "At home there is my mother, and we five girls. Father never returned from the Russian front and in the last days of the war they made my sixteen year old brother go to Berlin, and he never came home. My mother's heart is broken, she waited for him every day till she got that final letter. "We regret to inform you that your son has been killed in action." I have never heard my mother scream like that, her heart was broken."

"Killed!" she had wailed. "Whatever for? The war had been lost long before. Why did they have to take the young boys? He never held a gun, only to shoot rabbits." We have a farm hand now, he wandered in one day looking for work and Mother thought he looked a bit like my father and felt sorry for him. He works for his keep. He's a lazy ass, and I don't like the way he spies on me, always leering round corners."

Hubert is thinking to himself, 'If I can't have Audrey, maybe this is the answer. I need a wife to give me standing in the community and an incentive to work. She certainly seems softer than those snooty French girls back home. We might hate the Germans, but the war wasn't her fault. She's pretty brave though, it wasn't long ago that French girls had their hair shaved in the city square for fraternising with the enemy, stripped naked and their breasts daubed with Swastikas. There was that French actress Arletty, who, when she went on trial and was later imprisoned for treason, had famously said, 'My heart belongs to France, but my vagina is international.'

This girl is plucky, but will have to be thick skinned when she moves to France. The biggest question, though, is how will my parents react?

I bid her adieu; I tell her that I will come to the farm on my next day off. She skips down the meadow, off to milk the cows I presume. My feelings are all over the place. I have committed myself to a perfect stranger, am I mad?

Suddenly, I have to look at Audrey's photo which I carry in my breast pocket. She goes everywhere with me, day and night we are together. I look at her and wonder, what will she think of my marrying someone I don't even know? Look what you have done to me, Audrey! I have thrown caution to the wind.

'Oh, ma Cherie, Audrey,' I whisper. The sun is shining upon you, wherever you are, I am sure of it. One day I will see you again.

Please forgive me for making this decision. This union has nothing to do with you. Rest assured that nothing can ever change my feelings for you. Goodnight my love.

CHAPTER SIX

Heidi

"Why are you wearing your best dress?" my mother enquires, "It isn't Sunday."

"I just felt like it, it's such a lovely day," I tell her, trying to appear normal while bursting with excitement.

"Well, change into your work clothes, we have to make the rye bread and Daisy has to be milked."

"It's Klaus's turn to milk the cow. He's a lazy so and so, he just hides behind the shed and jumps out at me."

"Stop your moaning and get on with the chores," Mother says angrily.

I can hardly keep the excitement to myself, I even want to tell Daisy as I lean into her warm body and draw the milk from her teats. I think she would be pleased for me. Not so my sister Marie. She rushes to her bed and sobs when she hears my news. Her boyfriend Hans has not returned from the war; they were engaged, she even has a ring, she just keeps hoping. I wonder if I will have a ring one day.

The other sisters are horrified." A Frenchman?" they cry. "What nerve, you must be game."

I just shrug my shoulders, very smug in my latest venture. I don't mention that he is in love with another woman who he can't marry, so I just ignore that.

I have to find the right time to tell Mother. When I find her, she is in her usual chair by the stove, darning socks, I suddenly say, "I am going to marry a French soldier." She looks startled, then bursts out laughing.

"What do you mean, a Frenchman? You must be mad."

I tell her the whole story while my sisters look on in alarm.

"He could be a serial killer," my eldest sister suggests, rolling her eyes.

"He actually looks very nice, and I love the way he tries to speak German," I reply, very cross at the suggestion.

"When am I going to meet your future husband?" Mother asks.

"He'll come to the house on his next day off. Please be nice to him. You can't possibly know how much this means to me."

"Oh." She groans. "We'll have to wait and see. Oh, if only your father was here to see what this wild daughter of his has concocted."

I go to bed that night early, having so much to think about. I have nightmares about the war; food is still rationed, I am always hungry. At the end of the war, when the English heard that the

Germans were still short of food, they said "Let them starve." How can they be so cruel? Still, there was that lovely English soldier and the chocolate bar.

When the war began I would escape to the forest from an awful feeling of terror. It was on the face of everyone and the smell of corruption was in every corner. Dread was in every footstep, in the rustle of foliage, in the rattle of every horse cart, in every laugh or cry or shout, every minute of the day and night. Each time the doorbell rang you could see fear on people's faces.

I used to go to the forest with my friend Henri. One day we saw the white faces of little children staring at us. When we spoke, they did not answer but watched every step we made.

I ran home and told Mother. She said, "They are Polish children, torn from their mother's arms and made to chop wood and shovel coal from train wagons." That made me very sad; I knew it was wrong. As the war progressed the search for food became an obsession, none of the stark naked ruins of rubble created by the war affected us as hunger did. Most children stopped playing, just sat unsmiling and white faced. We would roam the streets searching for something edible in garbage bins, we became thieves and scavengers. The enemy was advancing, the sound of anti-aircraft guns, planes swooping and bombing came all night, we never knowing if they were friend or foe. Defeated soldiers trampled through the village desperate for food. Hunger overcame everything else. My eldest sister would disappear in the evening and come home at dawn with a bag of flour or biscuits. No one asked any questions, and we all swooped on the food like scavengers.

When we realised that the war was lost and the enemy was advancing, we were holed up in the cellar for days with a few

Limerence

chunks of rye bread. The gunfire was intense, and we could feel the vibration of the shells bursting. We were wide eyed as we realised our vulnerability but had to wait. A bit later we heard banging, kicking, on the cellar door. The noise, Bang! Bang! was terrifying.

"We will have to open it," my grandfather said sadly.

"Don't open it. No," my mother yelled, "We'll be raped."

"They're looking for weapons. They'll break the door down anyway," Grandfather answered as he opened the door.

We expected to see anger on the face of the enemy, but the soldier's features showed only compassion, maybe even grief. Then a smile broke over his face, and without a word he threw a bar of chocolate to me. I turned it over and over and shared it, my first chocolate for years.

We were able to return home, the soldiers and the red cross giving us food and clothes. There had been no school for some time, and I had become very ill with rheumatism. When I did return to school I was the object of ridicule, arms and legs like broom sticks, black stockings darned in whatever colour my grandmother could get her hands on.

Things gradually returned to normal although I never caught up with my school work and when I was fifteen I left to help my mother on the farm. I have put a bit of flesh on my bones, and think I look quite pretty. I must look okay, because Hubert said yes. I missed so much schoolwork that I hope he will understand. After the wedding I am going to live with him in the French town of Besçanon: it will be hard leaving my mother and sisters but I have to do it, there is no other way to escape.

"A dress, what am I going to do about a wedding dress?" I wail the next day. "We still need coupons to buy material and there isn't much around."

"Let me think about it. I'm actually quite excited to have a wedding in the family at last," Mutter says, a big smile on her face, so different from the day before. She is becoming more receptive to the idea.

My sister Hetty exclaims, "You know my friend Greta, well, I have been helping her around the house, and she tells me that there is a trunk in her attic that belonged to the Glickmans, you know; they had the garment factory, and Greta used to work for them."

"Yes," Mutter says, "I do remember them, they were very nice people, and they didn't come home. It is too awful to contemplate."

"Greta was saying that she thinks there will be lovely material in the trunk. I'll mention that we are going to have a wedding in the family and she might suggest that we have a look."

Greta is another war widow and her only son was called up in the last days of the war and never came home. She is a smart woman, having held an important job in the garment factory, but since the end of the war she has lost any incentive for living. She sells odds and ends at the market, mushrooms in season, and has eked out a living as best she can.

"I'll see her tomorrow at the market." Hetty is excited.

"Oh, would you? That would be marvellous, you can be my flower girl!" I fling my arms around her and go to bed dreaming of wedding dresses.

The following morning Hetty and I speak to Greta about my wedding plans. She seems very interested, and tells me what a fine family the Glickmans had been. She's sure that there will be lovely material in the trunk, and suggests we climb to the attic to investigate.

The room is musty, the trunk covered with thick dust that Greta wipes off, then produces a heavy key. All the time she talks about the Glickman family, how he was a kind and gentle man and a good teacher. Mrs Glickman was in charge of quality control and made sure nothing left the factory that had not been inspected thoroughly with her eagle eye. Their children had been clever at school, destined to be lawyers or doctors, until they were herded away in cattle trucks; not one had returned. Tears well in my eyes at the deep sadness of this reality, the human cost. Greta lifts the lid gingerly and removes the tissue paper covering the most exquisite materials, silk, satin and voiles.

"Mrs Glickman must have been saving these for her own daughter's wedding," Greta says as she lifts the first piece out.

I cannot believe my eyes, such beautiful fabrics. I choose a cream satin for the bridal dress and cream voile for the flower girl. As we explore the contents of the trunk a lace veil emerges, and in a box a carefully wrapped golden crown.

"Do you know," Greta says, "I remember a picture of their wedding in the dining room when they invited me for Friday Shabbat. I am almost sure that this was the veil and headdress that she wore. Oh, they are such happy memories," Greta sighs.

"I haven't done any sewing for ages, but I haven't forgotten how. I'd love to help you make it."

"Oh Greta, you are wonderful."

"That is the least I could do for my darling Henri's childhood friend." With tears in her eyes, she sets up her sewing machine that has lain idle for years and the room is soon a hive of industry with tape measures, scissors, patterns, threads, laughter and giggling girls; it is like the old days.

That evening mother bursts into tears at the sight of her daughter dressed in the most beautiful wedding dress she has ever seen.

"Oh darling, you look so beautiful. If only your father and brother could be here." We embrace each other, thinking about the adventures that await me, a little farm girl.

CHAPTER SEVEN

The Wedding

Hubert and his family arrive in Germany two days before the wedding, along with Hubert's friend Jacques who is to be the best man, and they book into a pension. They visit the farmhouse to meet the family, and communicate in a garbled mixture of French and German. There is lots of smiling, head nodding, and pleasantries enough, although no one knows that it was Heidi—not Hubert—who proposed the marriage. The undercurrent of French-German tensions is palpable, but no words are spoken, for this is a marital union of the highest order, and a French soldier is taking a bride sacred to all in the land, so cultural strains must be left at the door for this day.

Hubert's parents can clearly see that their son's upbringing is entirely different to that of his new bride; whereas their home is lined with books and academia is stressed, there is not a book to be seen in the farmhouse, only the heavy family bible.

Heidi is just a simple farmer's daughter, pretty and pleasant enough, but with very little to contribute in the way of knowledge; their concerns begin to grow as to how long she will be able to keep him interested without being his intellectual match, or at least able to keep up with big brain Hubert. Back at the pension, Hubert's mother looks concerned and ventures to say, "Heidi seems a very sweet girl, but I don't think you have much in common."

"Mother, we will work things out, I have made up my mind," Hubert replies gruffly. They know not to argue with their son; he has always had a particular mind and way about doing things, and they know better than to interfere further. Hubert's father knows that nothing has been mentioned since Hubert's last visit to Audrey, which he helped facilitate, so let sleeping dogs lie. Tomorrow is the civil ceremony in the town hall, and everyone goes to bed with their own thoughts, Hubert cradling the picture of Audrey, kissing her goodnight in his dreams, apologising over and over for marrying another. He tosses and turns all night, longing for Audrey and is feverish in the thought of what she would think of this. He tries to come to terms with the idea of Heidi in his arms, but he cannot, and visions of Audrey intrude at every turn.

The next morning Jacques looks at Hubert with a degree of consternation; he, more than anyone, understands Hubert's current state of mind and hastens to put a voice to it. Looking across the way to the farmhouse, then back to his friend, he asks, "Hubert, are you sure you are doing the right thing? I mean, one minute you are

Limerence

madly in love with Audrey, and the next minute you are giving your heart to a stranger?"

"Jacques, oh my dear friend, how can I make you understand? I am in love with a woman who has stolen my heart and whom I can't have. Heidi has come along and she is pretty keen to be married. I need a woman in my life to give me stability and purpose. I do not need to love her, but I like her; and since never again will I ever find a love like Audrey, I am prepared to settle, and this is enough."

"Well, that's a strange philosophy indeed; you are not leaving yourself open to the possibility of finding another girl you might fall in love with. Ever since your trip to England, since you met Audrey, you've changed, you have become sullen, serious; I tell you this as your best man out of true concern."

"Jacques, I understand your misgivings, but the depth of love I have for Audrey can never be duplicated. I go to bed every night with her in my arms—you just don't understand. I have to get on with my life now, I will marry. Just like Audrey, it is time for me to get down to business. We have to go to the town hall for the civic ceremony today, the Lord Mayor will be waiting."

Heidi's family are already at the town hall when Hubert's family arrive; everyone is dressed in their smartest outfit. Heidi's mother looks over enviously at the French couple, and, sad that her husband isn't there, thinks to herself that 'This war thing was so stupid—now we are all friends now. My men should be here.'

The ceremony is conducted very formally in German, while the Lord Mayor looks on, bored to death. Heidi is very sweet in national costume, her blonde plaits wrapped around her head. Jacques is grinning to himself, thinking,' maybe Hubert should be dressed in Lederhosen, 'but he manages to stay serious and produces the rings.

Heidi fingers her ring tenderly, looking up at Hubert expecting a kiss, but there is not one forthcoming. 'He is waiting for tomorrow at the real wedding, 'she thinks, comforting herself.

Hubert's father takes everyone to lunch, and there is an air of forced camaraderie, although Jacques is in his element, surrounded by the sisters, feeling almost spoiled for choice, free to have his pick of the women.

They return to their respective homes to prepare for the tomorrow's festivities, Heidi to spend her second last night in the farmhouse.

The wedding causes quite a sensation in the village, although not everyone agrees with the match. Nevertheless, the whole village turns out to see Heidi, the pretty girl everyone knows, marrying a handsome French boy. People gather outside the church; the bells ring lustily, echoing throughout the village. Everyone is smiling, Heidi glowing in the afternoon sun, a picture of pure happiness.

Hetty looks lovely in cream voile, hoping and praying that she will catch the bouquet and be the next to marry. The sisters have enjoyed dressing up and are proud of their inventive ways with such scant access to dress materials.

Maria is a sourpuss, somewhat understandably as she had never heard again from Hans. Heidi's mother is spruced up in her Sunday dress, and looks quite jaunty in a hat Greta found for her.

Outside the church Heidi stands like a statue, a bridal masterpiece, as her sisters affix the veil and golden crown around her blonde braids, cover her face, and tend to the light lace train. Her apple cheeks shine with happiness as she glances down at her heart shaped neckline, holding a simple bouquet of Lily of the Valley; a long white ribbon dangles from the sheath and dances in the light breeze.

Her wrist carries a satin pouch of bread and salt for prosperity. Heidi is floating in heavenly delight, dreamer she is; her wedding day is here, she has finally found a husband, he will provide a home and together they will make a family. It is the happiest dream of her life, to become somebody's wife.

Inside the church Hubert's parents are seated in the front right pew, looking smart as only the French do, trying to look pleased. Hubert's mother sports a lovely peach coloured suit bought before the war that she has hardly worn. His parents are a handsome couple; married young, they are barely middle-aged now. She has classic high cheekbones, an angular face, and her dark hair falls gently on her collar; he is handsome, like his son, dressed in a grey suit. He has a full head of hair, just a hint of distinguished grey at the temples.

In the opposite pew sits Greta, making sure that she has a good view of the bridal party to check that the hems are level. She reflects that Mrs Glickman would enjoy looking down on the bridal party, nodding and smiling approvingly. Next, Jacques rises to join his friend on the right, contemplating which sister to flirt with tonight. Hubert waits at the front and looks down the long aisle. He is a nervous wreck as all he can think about is Audrey.

The music starts and Hetty leads the procession as the flower girl, looking lovely in her cream voile three-quarter length dress, wearing a garland of flowers on her head. The bride follows and Hubert watches the procession make their way down the aisle towards him. All eyes are on Heidi, but he is in a momentary trance, imagining that under the veil is Audrey. She is coming to him as if in an apparition; he can feel the excitement grow, and his chest starts to pound at the thought that it could possibly be her, after all; her soft features, the look of love in Audrey's eyes as he lifts the veil to reveal his stunning bride.

"You may kiss the bride," the priest announces, interrupting his fantasy. He lifts the veil and looks at Heidi. She offers her lips; Hubert tries not to step backwards, lets go of her veil and awkwardly attempts to plant a kiss on her cheek. Heidi, disappointed, reaches out for his hand, but there is no feeling in it, no feeling at all.

The service is in German and Latin, a Catholic mass. The couple kneel at the altar and the groom puts his knee on the bride's veil to indicate that he will be the one in charge. Heidi stands and in return, steps on Hubert's foot playfully as to show that she will not be browbeaten. Mutti rolls her eyes in exasperation and cannot help whispering to herself under her breath, 'wilful child.'

Hubert leads his bride out of the church to cheers and applause all around. The couple are showered with rice which, when they stick to the head, symbolise the number of children they will expect. Everyone is smiling and happy. Hubert looks sick.

Outside the church a trestle table has been set up bearing a log of wood and a saw with handles at either end. As in German tradition, the bride and groom must set about sawing the log, as symbolic of their resolution to work together. Heidi begins sawing with such vigour she almost beats a wretched looking Hubert.

The wedding customs over, Hubert's eyes fill with tears of regret as the wedding party walks over the old cobblestones to the gaily decorated village hall for the wedding feast. The room is decorated in German style, lit with candles; Hubert imagines

Limerence

Audrey's nod of approval as he leads her to the bridal table to seat his queen.

Heidi gets ready to throw her bouquet; she understands the symbolism of luck and the promise of marriage. She tosses it over her left shoulder and has luck would have it Hetty captures the prize, and screams with delight. This means she will be the next in line for a proposal—but where are all the men?

Both German and French food and wine flow copiously, and everyone tucks into Hochzeitssuppe soup, German wedding soup, ending the evening with a Croquembouche, a French wedding cake which Hubert's Mother had persuaded the local baker to make, under her strict instructions.

Heidi eats heartily; Hubert picks at his food wishing the whole façade would come to an end and he could return to his happy place with Audrey.

There is dancing and the bride and groom touch for the first time apart from their kiss at the altar. They whirl around the room, Heidi in a dream-like state, Hubert wishing it were Audrey in his arms. Hetty asks Hubert to dance, and they waltz together smiling, not speaking as Hetty is nervous about her French. When the band stops playing, they look around the room to see the crowd has dispersed.

Hubert looks for his bride but she is nowhere to be seen. He waits awhile quite unconcerned, then enquires of his mother if she has seen her.

"While you were dancing with Hetty a group of men surrounded her and whisked her away. Apparently, that is the custom here, they have kidnapped her and you have to find her."

Hubert searches for Jacques who is surrounded by a group of giggling girls.

"Come on Jacques, you have to help me find my bride."

The pair wander through the village; Hubert knows the area well having been stationed there during the army of occupation. They light up their cigs Gauloises and circle around the marketplace to the town hall, the school, the baker, the butcher. Where would a good hiding place be? By this time the pair are getting tired, looking bedraggled, but notice a Shooting Hall down a side street.

They push open the door to see Heidi surrounded by her captors. They all return to the village hall where Hubert says goodnight to Heidi, almost calling her Audrey from all the alcohol he has consumed. How ironic, to be searching for the girl he least wants to find, and to not find the girl he most wants.

CHAPTER EIGHT

Heidi

The train trip is marvellous, exciting and my first real adventure. The country we pass through is beautiful, and, when we stop at the border, some men get on and ask to see our papers. Hubert tells me they are customs, that I don't need papers seeing as I'm his wife. I marvel at not having to worry about things like that.

I reach out to hold Hubert's hand, but he shrugs it off. Oh well, maybe it's considered rude, the French are so strange. The trip takes a few hours, and I doze, yesterday was so stressful and draining. Hubert's mother and father chat among themselves, addressing me occasionally in German. I am beginning to realise what it will be like when everyone around me speaks a different language. I'll have to work at learning the language which will please Hubert.

We reach the town of Besçanon, which is in a valley with a river running through it, and it looks beautiful in the afternoon light. My heart is beating wildly, and I pinch myself to make sure it's not a dream. It's just a short walk to the apartment that Hubert has found, and which he has taken pains to tell me about; he seems very proud of what he has done. So he should be, having me for a wife.

I wonder if he will carry me over the threshold and I look at him hopefully, but he unlocks the door and calmly walks in ahead of me. I'm so excited, my own little house. I set down my suitcase and explore. It has a small kitchen with a wood stove, a table, two wooden chairs and a couch that is a bit worn. My first job will be to try and patch that couch. There are a couple of saucepans, a frying pan and some cutlery. A large bed takes up most of the bedroom, and there is a white cupboard against the wall for our clothes. The bed has been made up with a puffy duvet, a wedding present from my parents-in-law; it looks quite cosy, I can't wait to jump in. There is a bathroom with an old bath and basin, and the toilet is outside. There is another small room looking over the fields with a desk, chair and typewriter.

"This is my study," announces Hubert. "I will probably be spending most of my time at home in this room. It is very small, but I can concentrate on my studies. I intend to be the top lawyer in town."

I'm not sure what a lawyer is, but it sounds important. My own home, it is a palace. I twirl around and scream with excitement. Hubert just says, "I am glad you like it," giving me a small smile.

I am nervous about going to bed tonight; my sisters have told me what is expected of me. I hope it is alright, that I am able to bear the pain they say will come. I find a nightdress, a long cotton one which came out of Mrs Glickman's trunk; it covers me from head to toe. I undress hurriedly without so much as a glance from Hubert, and I slip into bed with my new husband. He has turned away from me and is already breathing heavily and so I lie still and wait. Nothing happens and he starts to snore. He hasn't kissed me yet, I suppose that will come. I lie in the darkness with a man next to me for the first time in my life. He is warm and large next to the small of my back and I want to touch him, stroke his hair, kiss his lips. But nothing. I turn my wedding ring in time to his snores. I am a married woman. I wonder if it is all a dream.

I am already awake when he stirs. I put my fingers on his cheek, but he turns away quickly, rolls out of bed without a word and goes to the bathroom. Oh well, I didn't think it would be like this, so I get dressed and go to the kitchen. There's good supplies, his mother said she had shopped before they left, so I make some heferschrott, which I think the French call farine, and am sitting eating it with brown sugar and cream when he comes in.

"What's this?" he asks, so I tell him." It is what we have for breakfast, it was in your cupboard." I hand him some on my spoon, and after a moments hesitation, he puts it in his mouth, then grins. I haven't seen him do this before, and I suddenly see how handsome he actually is.

"Ah, farina, the English porridge. This is very nice." He fills a bowl and eats. "Thank you, Heidi, I'm glad you like cooking. I will have steak for dinner."

He gets up and disappears, soon returning with a big leather satchel, and leaves. Not another word. I shrug. 'Well, you wanted to get married, 'I tell myself, and get ready to explore the apartment and the town.

There's two one hundred franc notes on the dresser. He must have left them for the shopping, but what do I need, where do I get it, and how much will this buy? All questions I am going to get answers to soon, I suspect. Managing a household is something we were all trained to do. I am looking forward to this, it will help me forget my mother and our way of life. 'German women are tough,' my mother used to say. 'We have to be.' I'm twenty. I'll show them. But my heart is pounding with anxiety.

I put on my coat, woollen hat, gloves and leather boots and venture out. It's freezing cold, just like home, and there's no one in the street. I walk to the corner and look at the Strasse, there's a sign saying "l'étoile" on the lamp post, and pointing to the right. I look and realise that this is a big town. Probably a city. I start towards it.

I come to the market in the cross street: big, noisy, with produce fresh from the farms, orchards and rivers. I've never seen anything like it. Bright people everywhere talking so fast I cannot understand even one word. There is no fresh food in the house and I have brought my big cloth carry bag, Mother gave me hers. I pick up a bunch of fresh carrots and hold it up.

"How much?" I ask in my halting French.

"Boch?" The stall lady says with a sneer.

"Ja." So I ask her in German, and she growls. She doesn't like me, but when I hold up the bank note it's as if the sun has broken through the clouds.

Before I know it my bag is full, and other stall holders are pushing me, trying to get me away from this one, but the lady yells at them—I'm sure she was swearing—then takes the note and hands me a few coins in change. She has overcharged me, I am certain—but I do not care.

Limerence

Further on I see a butcher's shop, all kinds of meat on display, but I only recognise sausages, which is what we mostly ate in Germany, apart from some hares we trapped. I go in, and the butcher gives me a friendly smile.

"Bonjour Madam, qu'est-ce que vous desirez? What do you desire?"

I can understand a few French words, and I get the sense of what he has said. I look at the cuts of meat. I am looking forward to cooking for my husband and I know that French food is much lighter than the standard heavy German dishes of meat and potatoes. I point to a nice pink round piece of meat; I can feel myself blushing. The butcher gives me a big grin and answers in German.

"This is an excellent cut of filet mignon, and if served with champignon and wine, it makes a fine dinner for any man." He has a nice smile, is charming and polite, not heavy and gruff like the big men back home. I blush again and reply. It is suddenly refreshing to speak my native tongue again.

After we have talked a while and I have told him my story, (though not about me asking to be married), he tells me that the Bisset family is well known, and I will be respected in the town. This is a relief, and I am glad to hand my money over. He wraps my selections in white paper which he ties with string. I am smiling with happiness as I leave.

My sisters had warned me that some people would be hostile, and told me to be brave and ignore them. Word travels fast in a small town, and as I return home many of the women stare at me. Who is this new young woman? A German? We'll soon put her right. But many smile, some nod and others turn away. In time they will get to know me.

German potato pancakes with bratwurst are on the dinner menu for tonight. Every day I will learn a new word; I get out the dictionary my sisters gave me, as I would like to impress Hubert. He is, I suppose, a very serious person, but he just has to get to know me better.

Towards evening I set the table, make the pancake mix and light a candle, straighten up the room, change my dress and wait for Hubert to come home. I sit on the couch and dream as I imagine our family future; babies, birthday parties, a nice home and pretty garden, my sisters coming to visit and being quite envious of my perfect life. I fall asleep waiting for Hubert to come home. He bangs open the door and I wake with a start.

"How was your day?" I ask, a mixture of German and French.

He nods, then says, "I'll wash then have my dinner."

I begin cooking, then serve the meal; it looks lovely, I find some mustard and some butter.

I am about to start eating, I am quite hungry, when Hubert says gruffly, "I ordered steak."

My heart sinks. "I did buy it, but don't know how to cook it. I'll find out and you will have it tomorrow. Sorry."

I watch him eating his first supper, he seems to be enjoying it.

"Hmm," he says, "this is nice. You are a good cook."

We drink wine with our meal and I try to make conversation about my day and shopping, but he doesn't seem interested. He rises from the table, thanks me for the lovely dinner and disappears into his office. I clear up, do the dishes, sit and knit and think of home. I wonder who is milking the cow and who Klaus is annoying now. I am feeling sleepy, so get ready for bed.

He comes out of his office, undresses and joins me under the sheets. He turns the light off and I am thinking, is this going to be our first married night? He kisses me on the cheek and before I know it, he is pushing up my nightdress, then busily manoeuvring himself around on top of me. I do not know what I am expected to do.

I feel his closeness, but it seems business like, as though he is hell bent on a certain task. He touches my breasts, then he is entering me. Oh dear, it hurts, I cry out. He apologises, rolls off me and gives me a peck on the cheek. It feels messy; I lie there mystified. Is that what it is all about? I certainly did not enjoy it, but Hubert is snoring in no time. I lie awake for what seems hours, staring at the ceiling.

Hubert sleeps like a log, then bounces out of bed in the morning, not a word about the night before, and gobbles his porridge and disappears for the day. I go to make the bed and see the bloodied sheets. Oh dear, is this what it is supposed to be? I wish I had someone to talk to, maybe I will meet another woman in town and we can be friends. I am missing my mother and sisters terribly and can't wait for the postman's whistle. I find myself crying, I can't help it, is this what they call homesickness? After a few minutes I dry my eyes and give myself a talking to.

"This is what you wanted girl; you have to make the most of it. Hubert seems a serious man but he will get to know me better.

CHAPTER NINE

Hubert

I travel from Besçanon to the University of Lille twice weekly, working on my post-doctoral studies. I am heavily involved with my professional duties as a lawyer as well as seeking tenure at the university, hopefully as professor. My sexual passions have evaporated, Audrey being a glowing shadow in my heart. I have been married for some years now but rather than converse with my wife, I resort to my office, gazing forlornly at my darling's picture, dreaming about what my life might have been.

I know Heidi would dearly love a baby, just as I would, but she has had no less than four miscarriages and I am sure she will not agree to trying again; the doctor says it was probably the deprivations she experienced during the war that caused them. Both our parents can't help hoping, and mine keep dropping hints; her sisters call and urge her on, but she has gone through such pain and distress that I did not have the heart to press her. However, just ten weeks ago she said to me, tears in her eyes, "Come on, let's try one more time. My need is greater than yours."

Now, by a miracle, she is carrying our child. I thank God, pray to the Virgin to protect her every night. She is becoming radiant, positive, and the change is remarkable. Already pretty, she is now a rejuvenated flower, and I am happy.

She speaks French very well but will never lose the German accent; she has made friends with a few people, one in particular. I urge her to rest more and offer to help with the shopping, but she ignores me. She telephones her mother with the news of the pregnancy; I can hear the squeals of delight from the sisters, they all want to be aunties. Her mother wants to come here immediately, but the farm is in full production and she has to remain there.

I have found a much bigger apartment and had some men come in to fix it up to my liking; it has a nice nursery, a decent study and a sunny lounge room.

I am so excited at the prospect of becoming a father, but can't help wishing it were Audrey who were carrying my baby. My fantasies look foolish when I realise she is more likely to be having children to another man. That letter she wrote. I will never get over it, but every year, on the same date I received it, I record the event in a little note book.

I relax in my old leather chair, allow my thoughts to drift to Heidi once more. She is a good wife, liked by our neighbours and my parents, but I can never get Audrey out of my mind. No matter how hard I try, or what I do, her image is before me all the time.

I hear Heidi knock on the door as she brings me an aperitif. I watch in pure fascination as she walks across the room, imagining that it is Audrey floating across the room, shimmering in the light, skirt dancing around her thighs.

I light a cigarette, pick up my pen and begin to write.

Besçanon, September 1963

My dearest Audrey,

I am alone in my office. Suddenly I have to look at your photo. The sun is shining wherever you are. I want to dial your number and hear your voice just once. I wonder how your marriage is going with the Swiss man. Mine flounders in the ocean like a dead corpse, never to end, just floating pointlessly out to sea. I miss you, my dear. It is a hole in my heart that can never be filled. I lack your touch, I lack your smile, I wish we could just be, awhile.
Yours ever faithfully,

Hubert.

CHAPTER TEN

Heidi

Hubert left for Lille this morning by the early train, planning to be away for two days. I am eight and a half months pregnant, round and bouncy as a beach ball; my back hurts but I don't mind, my baby is worth any amount of pain. I look down at the bulge and wonder how long I have.

Late in the afternoon I feel a gushing sensation, and realise my waters have broken. I call my neighbour to ring Hubert's mother, who arrives fifteen minutes later, bundles me into her car and takes me to the hospital. She rings her son with the news, and he says he will come immediately. I hope and pray he makes it in time.

I soon understand why they call it labour; it is such pain, like no other ever. It goes on and on until, after what seems a lifetime, the mid-wife announces that she can see dark hair. A few more pushes, then the words, "It's a girl!"

A feeling of relief comes over me, it has to be experienced to be believed. Hubert comes bursting through the door with his arms full of flowers, we are both crying with joy, except he doesn't kiss me. Oh my. If only my mother and sisters could be here to share this moment.

She is adorable, we have already chosen the name for a girl: Juliette. We both gaze at our little girl with wonder. When they put her to my breast it is quite a procedure, we both struggle, but, eventually she firmly latches on.

I cannot help gazing at this miraculous little girl. God heard my prayers at last, and I feel humble and overwhelmed, I nurse her and feed her and get some sleep when she does.

Hubert's mother comes and I say, "I have been looking at this baby for a whole day, and I am not bored." She smiles and adds, "You never will be, and neither will I. Thank you for giving us our first grandchild. You have been through so much, but you never gave up. You have the will to succeed, and the courage. I'm so pleased you are my daughter-in-law."

I can't wait to take her home, to her own room filled with so many baby clothes and toys. It is four days before they let me leave, there are no complications, no difficulties, she is perfectly healthy, and I am overjoyed. I carefully write down every change in my baby's life, and when, on the fourteenth day her eyes focus on me, it is a thrilling moment.

Hubert is away every day except Sunday. The birth took a lot out of me, I haven't been myself since. Getting up in the night to

Limerence

feed, Hubert snoring on. He is arriving home earlier in the evenings hoping to catch her before she is settled for the night.

I love being a mother, but it is lonely. It is hard to make friends with French women; they can never forget I am German. Hubert tells me not to worry, they are all snobs. But I have made one special friend, Françoise, who is kind and full of information. We walk to the park while her little girl rides her bicycle.

Hubert bounces Juliette on his knee when he gets home, we mark every milestone and I long to show her to my family. I had thought that once we had a baby, he might treat me more tenderly, but his feelings for me are unchanged. I so long for a bit of romance in my life. I have been talking to Françoise about his coldness; of course she does not know the whole story. She suggested that I create a romantic atmosphere and try to seduce him. I laugh at the very thought, but maybe she has a point and I hatch a plan.

Tonight I will put Juliette to bed early, make Hubert's favourite dish, a coq au vin, put on a dress I know he admires, and light a couple of candles. The scene is set. He comes home as usual, disappointed that Juliette is in her cot. I explained that she was a bit fractious, teething, and needed to be settled down. He sits down at the table, shakes his napkin, pours the red wine. I serve dinner quietly; he eats heartily, in silence as always, not a word about the candles, my dress or choice of menu. I have made his favourite desert, crème brûlée. Oh yes, I have been perfecting my French cuisine over the years, I even speak good French now.

He eats his dessert in silence, finishes his wine, politely folds his napkin, and is about to rise from his chair. I cannot contain myself.

"You selfish bastard, Hubert—am I just a servant to you?" He looks up shocked. "You haven't even noticed my dress, the candles, your favourite dish."

I slap his face hard. He reels in fright, touching his face.

He reels backwards, muttering, "But, I thought you were content, I have given you a nice home." He strokes his red face.

'And that is all,' I think, but say," Content, content, how could I be, all these years? I cook, clean, suffer your coldness. Have you forgotten, I am your wife?" I scream this at the top of my voice and Juliette starts to wail. "You treat me like a well worn door mat."

"You got what you wanted, which was to be a wife." He says this as though I am stupid.

"Yes, I did, but at what price? I am your servant, housemaid, you were quite ready to marry me, but you have turned out to be so selfish that my life is a misery." I am a red-faced, a shrill Haus Frau now, and I see his expression soften.

There is a long pause, and then he says softly, "I'm sorry Heidi, I will try to be more thoughtful." He smiles ingratiatingly. "Can I make coffee tonight?"

"Do as you like, you pompous ass." I storm out and pick up my whimpering baby. She is my delight, my comfort.

He makes the coffee, pours himself a whisky, even washes and dries the dishes; it is the first time this has ever happened.

We go to bed early, and as usual he rolls over without a word. All signs of caring for me disappeared the day we came back from the wedding. It's hard to even be in the same bed.

The next morning the air is cold, the atmosphere colder, and we go about our routine in deadly silence. He is distant, and this is probably how it will be from now on. It is as if a sheet of ice has formed between us.

Limerence

Then he takes me by surprise. "I am sure you would enjoy a trip to Germany to visit your family."

I nod and turn away from him, tears rolling down my cheeks into the soapy sink water. Hubert is clueless and never notices when I cry; he is the absent-minded professor, while I play the meek and mild obedient wife. He gets up from the table, kisses Juliette and leaves without another word. I watch him through the window; I really am past caring. I scoop up Juliette and get her ready, it's bath time.

I start to think that the butcher is looking sexier every day. He hands me the cut of meat across the counter as he usually does on Mondays, and today I hold his gaze a split second longer than usual, then leave with a warm smile. What would Hubert think if I had affair? I doubt if he would care. On the other hand, he would not like me to bring shame on the family, on such an important man in the town. But now the question is: do I care?

When I was sorting the laundry last week an old black and white photo of a girl dropped out of his shirt pocket. She had fair wavy hair and was smiling directly at the camera. My God! This has to be her, the other woman. I flop down in a chair, staring at the woman he could not marry, the woman whose invisible presence has been the cause of the distance between us. What do I do? Tear it to shreds or taunt him with it? I slide it under my bra and continue with the washing.

The following morning, as I am waiting in line at the butcher's, I take another look at the picture. I'm suddenly at the front of the line, and look up. He's not bad looking guy, wavy black hair, cute smile and dimples on each cheek. He asks me what I'd like, telling me to take my time and choose carefully. He smiles at me, winks. I think he is trying to flirt with me. I feel myself blushing, I must get out of here, they say butchers are highly sexed, all that red meat. My French is good now, but not good enough to hide the stammer emerging from my lips, caused by a sudden rush of blood.

"Je voudrais le filet mignon, s'il vous plaît."

Limerence

CHAPTER ELEVEN

Juliette

Papa and I often go out on our bicycles together in the countryside when it is a nice day. He carries the picnic lunch that Mama prepares for us, though she never comes, preferring to stay home.

We ride along the country roads without a care in the world and play games along the way; we say 'Moo' when we see a cow, 'Neigh' when we see a horse.

Papa makes a funny sound when we see a chicken which makes us laugh. Papa loves birds and knows all their names, he said as a boy he used to collect bird's eggs. We stop at pretty picnic spots along the way and pick wild flowers to take a posey home to Mama.

I love school, especially mathematics and languages. German is a breeze as Mama often speaks it at home though Papa is very keen for me to speak English. We study the arts and music, I play the piano sometimes and Papa sings. Although he loves classical music best, he has taken me to pop concerts. My parents never holiday together; Mama goes to Germany and used to take me when I was little, but now Papa and I holiday together. A few years ago we went to Switzerland, what a beautiful country it is.

Travelling by train, I could not sit still in my seat. I rushed from one side of the train to the other in awe, the highest snow-capped mountains on one side, and glistening ice-blue lakes on the other. We visited the black bears in a big pit in the middle of Bern, which is where the town gets its name. It did seem a bit cruel to me. There is talk of getting them a better habitat.

We went on the funicular railway; there was still snow on the mountains even though it was the middle of summer; we even visited a big house with a lovely garden. Papa knocked on the door which was answered by a girl wearing an apron, she could have been a maid. I saw three children inside and would have liked to play with them, but we weren't invited in. Papa asked for the lady of the house, but was told she was away for the day. I remember he quickly grabbed me by the hand and asked for the French Embassy. The maid looked confused and suggested the city, Basel. He seemed particularly quiet that day, saying the Swiss were a boring race.

Other years we went hiking in the Alps, or drove down to the Cote d'Azure for a week of beach and sun. We stayed in little apartments in the quiet town of Frejus, away from the glitzy towns of Antibes, Cannes and Saint Tropez, because it was simple and they had tennis courts which was his favourite sport; he is very good. He is patiently coaching me, but I will never be a good as he is. Papa reads a lot and encourages me to do the same. Mama doesn't read much, she makes the excuse that the war interfered with her schooling, although she is making an effort now and has and joined a book group.

When I was growing up, I didn't have much trouble dealing with exams at school and at college. I love studying, both my parents encourage me, and Mama often says, 'I wish I had had the opportunities that you have had. 'I feel lucky, but I wish we could do things as a family more. Papa has bought another house, a large house with a lovely garden. He loves antique furniture and is busy filling it with beautiful things. Mother is not at all interested, says she hates old things, the house is too big and away from her friends. Papa bought her a smaller house near the market and a park where she can walk her dog. It seems to be working out well.

Papa is very busy with his legal practice and establishing a law faculty at the university in our town. Mother comes to the big house each day and prepares a meal for him, but is happy to leave 'all this old junk, 'as she calls the antiques. He fills his house with books, furniture he buys from auction rooms. He is getting a bit of a paunch now and his hair is thinning, but to me he is the most handsome man. He also enjoys his garden, and is very proud of the roses. This is how we live, in two houses; it is hard to explain to my friends, but I say that they have different tastes and everyone is happier.

Now I am making my way as a junior litigator fresh out of college. Living away from home during the week, I look forward to returning home at the weekends and to the smell of mother's cooking, and where Papa and I talk well into the night, me forever plying him with legal questions. He has his lawyer friends over occasionally, they play cards and drink well into the small hours. He is so happy. When Papa and I go on holidays we make a point of visiting all the best art galleries: the Rijks Museum in Amsterdam, the London Tate, and I visit the Louvre often now that I'm living in Paris. We are so lucky living in Europe. Everything is at our fingertips.

Papa asks me when I am going to bring a boyfriend home. I haven't met anyone yet that really interests me.

Last night he announced, "Mother is joining us for dinner tonight, wear a nice dress. I have booked a restaurant." He takes a little note book out of his pocket, and seems to be staring into the past and scribbles something in the book. I enquire.

"What is that all about?"

"Oh, nothing, I just remembered what date it was." He seems to be lost in his own thoughts.

Mama arrives early, as she always does, and fusses about the kitchen tidying up. She looks very nice tonight in a black dress and smart shoes. Her hair is greying but she always wears it in a neat Chignon, and I call her the consummate smart French lady of fashion. I wish Papa would complement her on the way she looks sometimes. She endeavours to live up to the image of a judge's wife.

We enjoy a quiet dinner at a homely French bistro, family cooking of the French Comte region. Mama enjoys the local Morteau, a smoked pork sausage and saucisse montbeliard, the oldest sausage to be found anywhere in France, whilst Papa partakes of his favourite Coq au vin which Mama also makes for him at home. He sometimes cries over the fondue, especially when it is made with the local Comte cheese. Mama reminds him that it will clog up for his arteries. Papa groans, but knows she is right. I have the Coq au Vin, mindful that it will never beat Mama's. Papa orders absinthe and insists that we order a special dessert.

After dinner we return home; Papa pours a cognac. Mama wants to leave, saying she has to care for her dog. Papa insists she not go out in the cold night air.

"Nonsense! We survived harsher conditions than this in the war," she says with a bite in her tongue. The air feels thick, I fear a fight is brewing, but it stops when they look at me. Mama wraps a scarf round her neck and kisses me softly on the cheek wishing me goodnight, and safe travels back to Paris. She turns, offers her cheek to Hubert for a parting kiss, leaving Papa and myself to our night conversations and political rambles.

"Anything wrong with you and Mama?" I ask pointedly, feeling a bit of bravado with the wine.

"Nothing for you to worry about, my sweet child," Papa says and pours himself another cognac.

"Now, where were we? You were about to tell me about your new boyfriend?" He needles me playfully and we both watch the flames of the fire.

Out of the blue he suddenly says, "Make sure you marry for love." I look at him; he looks sad. I have noticed that Papa gets breathless when we walk far, and suggest he make an appointment with his doctor. He rubs his chest bone, dismissing my concerns with a pffft sound and a wave of the hand, insisting he is fine, but I will keep at him.

CHAPTER TWELVE

Hubert

I'm on my own now, and very lonely. For an intelligent man I've lived an unloving life, locked in the impossible dream of a young and foolish man. I have ignored my wife, treated her like dirt, made her unhappy and sad. I wonder if it is a form of madness, this fetish, if the next life will be the same, pining away somewhere without hope. Prestige and honour are no substitute for affection. If only I could reclaim the exuberance of youth.

I really live for my daughter now, who is quick and smart. She loves me without reservation; she is patient, cajoling, and brilliant. She has Heidi's blue eyes and a German will of steel. She will do

Limerence

well in the law, for that is her calling. I am so proud of her. Whatever love I denied Heidi I have poured into Juliette.

Heidi and I have dinner every week, we talk about politics and current affairs, my work, our daughter. I must admit to not being as fit as I used to be, age I suppose; I have health issues with my heart, hoping medication will fix it. I wonder, is it possible to die from a broken heart?

I am tired of travelling to Lille and have handed in my tenure. I am busy with my private practice and my name is in the hat to perform judicial duties for the town, presiding as Judge of Besçanon.

If only I could share my successes with Audrey. What if I tried to find her, where could she be? Switzerland? England? What if I find her, will she want me? She may have even died?

I am plagued by the barrage of 'what ifs' to the point of being sick. In desperation I begin searching for her name in Switzerland, assuming that she may still be there. Of course it is hopeless. It occurs to me that I may be able to get information through her family name in Manchester, and being in the law it is quite easy. I ascertain which solicitors had been in business in that era, and after a few phone calls, I am making progress. Her surname was not a common one, so this has helped, and I have her home address from her letters.

I think I have made a coup. I have discovered her family solicitor in Manchester, and through him, her address. She now lives in the States with an address in California. I wonder if she is once again single. I hope against hope. I wonder what happened with the Swiss guy? I remember it was a charming house that he had provided for her, and as I peeped down the hall I saw all the English memorabilia, a brass warming pan and a hunting horn. I wonder how she would go decorating her American house. My mind is running away with me again. If I had bumped into her that day when we were both younger, finding that she was unhappy, maybe we would have connected again. I must stop dreaming. It gets me nowhere, but I seem powerless to do anything else.

Heidi came to dinner tonight; we don't have much to talk about. I asked her what she is reading, what television programs she is watching. It is all superficial. Her mother died recently and she is quite depressed. I often wonder if she regrets proposing to me. Was it cruel of me to expect a woman to live side by side for a lifetime without love? Only once did she lose her cool and slap me when Juliette was a baby. She still looks pretty good, not too many wrinkles, she must be tinting her hair, it isn't as grey as mine. She has developed a French dress sense, I give her a good clothes allowance and she always looks smart.

I wonder if she has entertained other men, had an affair. I wouldn't blame her, although it wouldn't look good, the wife of a judge having a secret affair. I think she must have, she looks too happy. I pray that she had the decency to be discreet.

Do I have the nerve to ring Audrey, now I have the phone number? It's past seven o'clock there, and Americans eat early; maybe she's watching television. I have a quick nip of cognac to steady my nerves. I will have to speak English; a female voice answers the phone. I feel weak, my hands are trembling.

"Hello, Hello, is that Audrey?"

"Speaking."

"This Hubert, Hubert Bisset from Besçanon speaking. We met at the 1948 Olympic Games. Do you remember?"

"Just a minute, I have to sit down." She sounds breathless. Oh my! My heart is pounding.

"Don't you remember me? I was a volunteer like you, we met at the opening ceremony; we danced, went to the cinema, you showed me all the sights."

"You will have to give me a minute. Yes, Hubert, I vaguely remember, but how on earth did you get my number, and why are you calling me?"

"I remembered your surname and that you came from Manchester. I got your number from your late Father's solicitor."

"My goodness, there has been a bit of sleuthing here."

"Well, I am in the law, one can find out these things."

"I often wonder how life has been for you?" I say.

Audrey hesitates, then says, "I divorced, moved from Switzerland to England for a few months, then met my American husband. He is a nuclear scientist, and we came to California."

"How do you find it, do you like it there?" I'm gabbling, my heart fluttering like a bird in a cage.

"It did take a while, but now I love it. The climate is perfect, I taught at a girl's private school, but now we are retired and love to travel."

"Did you teach the History of Art? I remember we talked about the French impressionists."

"I did, I also taught English literature, I introduced American schoolgirls to the classics."

"I imagine you were very good at that."

"Yes, the girls loved it, some have contacted me since and thanked me for introducing them to the world. I even received a postcard from a girl who had visited the Louvre and was grateful for the insight it had given her in the appreciation of art."

"How I envy you, I have a heart condition and am unable to travel far. Would you please send me a postcard the next time you go away? My address is Hubert Bisset, Rue de Linen, Besçanon, France." There is no reply.

I sigh. "It has been lovely talking to you, I have often thought about the happy times we had in London."

"Goodbye Hubert, thank you for calling."

Her voice! Her voice, it ... I burst into tears. My Audrey. I can't believe it. As I recover, I think back to our conversation. She spoke impeccable English. No trace of an American accent. Poor girl, she hasn't a clue how much she has featured in my thoughts. I long for her more than ever, and I should be realistic, put away these foolish desires. But I can't. There's no way I can let her go, this girl who captured my heart all those years ago. My lifetime companion, but only in my mind. Maybe there's something wrong with me. I don't care. I kiss her photo, and my own tears along with it.

CHAPTER THIRTEEN

Hubert

As a judge I sit on high every day, the accused and their lawyers below me in the body of the court room. I listen to them, talk to them, even smile sometimes, but in the end I have to uphold the law, decide who is right and who is wrong, who gets locked up and who goes free?

What is freedom, anyway, when I have a life sentence of unrequited love? It is worse than any I could ever deliver. It is this that sits like a stone on my heart, interfering with my concentration.

This morning I shower and dress quickly as I have to be at the courthouse by eight. Some days my court seems nothing but a drive-through confessional, a pit stop for those who have lost their way. We all make mistakes, and mine is Audrey. We get the day's proceedings under way, and I must concentrate. Audrey's voice rings in my ears.

"Your Honour, if you will pardon me, may I repeat the question? It seems you may not have heard me the first time."

"Let the record state the defendant pleads not guilty in the case of Ezequel versus Chopart," the attorney drones on. "May the deliberations now rest with the Court."

"Your Honour..." This time I sit up, attentive. I will need a transcript in order to digest the facts. I look at the accused, a kid about seventeen, young and scraggy looking, too thin, dressed in an ill-fitting suit, probably borrowed.

I vaguely recall some of the facts. "I must remind you, young man, that you are under oath. Do you wish to say anything in your defence before I impose a sentence?"

I beckon him to come forward; he approaches the bench nervously and whispers, "Your Honour, I know I have done wrong. I did break and enter her house, but it was only to see her. We had just broken up, her parents did not want me seeing her anymore, they think that we are too young to be in love—but I love her!" That was a cry I knew all too well. "I was not there to do her any harm. I just wanted to see her, I thought I could talk some sense into her. We were talking about running away together to be married, it was meant to be..."

His voice trails off, I can see that he is telling the truth, his eyes are sad, watery, pleading. I look at him, I understand his desperation, his longing, his loss. My mind drifts and I think of the last time I touched Audrey.

Limerence

The young man shrugs hopelessly, I understand his life sentence. It is mine.

"You do understand that breaking and entering is illegal?" I look at him sternly. How can I condemn him for doing what I want to do? "However, you did not steal anything, for that would be a felony."

The young man opens his mouth and gasps, then sneaks a quick glance over his shoulder towards the gallery where she is sitting with her parents, and it is there I see the object of his infatuation. She tries a half hopeful smile in his direction. She's a pretty girl, young and fresh faced, dark silky curls and soft sweet sweet doe eyes. They are just two innocent, stupid kids in love; there is no criminal intent here.

I want to tell these kids to run away, elope, get married, follow your heart's desire. Do not second guess, just live. Be foolish, be impetuous, be reckless for a while, throw caution to the wind, fill your sails with hope and adventure and danger of the unknown!

But I am a judge and so I tell him, "What you have done is wrong, and you know this. I am sentencing you to a good behaviour bond, which will mean that you will not be able to approach or speak to the young lady without parental permission."

I stand. "This court is now adjourned." I turn and walk out.

I quietly hope, for his sake, she does not fall in love with someone else.

CHAPTER FOURTEEN

Hubert

I have decided to take a holiday, go to California and see for myself. All my research has at last paid off. Heidi is happy, she will go to Germany to see her family again. Juliette is so engrossed with her studies she just smiled at my decision. This is one trip I want to make on my own. My flight is direct to San Francisco and it departs at six o'clock.

Heidi is under the impression that I am a visiting a Fellow of Stanford University, invited to attend some faculty or other. Juliette is thrilled that I have taken her advice and put judicial responsibilities on hold for a week, citing personal reasons. I was somewhat afraid that she would want to come with me, but luckily, she didn't ask.

Limerence

    I sit in the club lounge at Charles De Gaulle airport; as I am not one for having much fashion sense, my bag is lightly packed with two shirts, a blazer, a spare pair of trousers and some underwear— in my impulsive state I could not care less what to pack anyway, the only reason for my travelling is to see Audrey.

    I wonder what I'll do when I finally see her. I feel like a giddy school boy as I take a sip of wine, seeing the reflection of a greying middle-aged man with wrinkles. I wonder if she will fancy me, find me attractive. I take another sip of wine as Etta James sings to me through the speaker set behind the bar.

> *At last my love has come along,*
> *My lonely days are over and life is just a song.*
> *At last, the skies above are blue*
> *My heart is wrapped in clover,*
> *the night I looked at you.*
> *I found a dream that I could speak to,*
> *A dream to call my own.*
> *You smiled, you smiled,*
> *and then the spell was cast.*
> *And here we are, for you are mine at last.*

    The flight is uneventful, and I eventually fall asleep, thankful for it being a red eye flight; a few wines and some mediocre food, Bach on my headphones, and I feel more relaxed than I have done for many years. So here I am, disembarking on the west coast of America and wondering what I am doing here. What I have done suddenly becomes very real to me; part of me wants to go back through customs and return home, but most of me wants to stay.

I walk through the departure lounge and follow the signs in English to the taxi rank. It is strange to see everything in English, it reminds me that I am not safely at home, but in a foreign land. The whole thing seems surreal; my English is not so good anymore, compared with the days when I travelled a lot. I see a man standing by his cab and wait to make eye contact. "Bon— sorry, hello," I say in halting English.

"Where y'all headed to man?" The taxi driver asks. He is a big burly guy with a drawl as long as his beard, which tells me that he is not from these parts, probably a southerner. His oversized gut hangs over the top of his pants, too much fried chicken, probably spends all of his life in his car, like most Americans. I give him the address in Los Gatos; he reminds me that it is peak hour and the 101 gets pretty jammed round this time of day. I am listening to his twang and it grates on my ears. I climb into the cab and once more become hopelessly wrapped up in the thought of Audrey, imagining she is sitting in the back of the taxi with me. It is thirty-one years and four months since I have seen this girl. Butterflies are swimming out of my ears and eyes, in my arms and down my spine. I have not felt this in three decades.

We merge into the five lane parking lot that is Highway 101 as Big Stan blasts his horn at another guy trying to push in. We crawl in dense traffic, the sun is glaring but it is surprisingly cool. I can't remember being so nervous before, not even in a courtroom. Big Stan careens left, he says we should take the University Avenue exit at Palo Alto, because it will be less congested. I silently nod and wave him onwards. I remember that Palo Alto is home to the Ivy League, Stanford University. They do have a great law faculty but I have never been there. I ask Big Stan if we can stop on the main shopping street; I would like to buy Audrey some flowers.

"Good idea man—great way to impress a lady, that what you're here for? You little French guys, you're big romantics over there, big lovers, eh? That's what they say, I dunno, you frogs," he says, and goes back to picking the food between his teeth. We stop on the main road that is University Avenue; kids are criss-crossing the street, arms filled with binders and folders, carrying their latest gadgets, and I step into the florist on the corner and ask for thirty-one white roses, one for every year we have been apart. I jump back in the taxi and ask Big Stan how far away we are. He says we have a good twenty minutes to go to Los Gatos, and we turn right onto Middlefield Road, taking us through the suburban town of Silicon Valley. I wince as the taxi meter clocks over; I want to say something, but feel I cannot. In our culture back home, although we like to complain about certain things, we also accept our lot in life. So I say nothing until Big Stan says it for me.

"Man, this sure as hell is gonna be a big fare—as big as me. Good for me I suppose, but bad for you, huh? Didn't you know where Los Gatos is? Almost next door to the ritzy village of Saratoga. Would'a been cheaper if you had flown direct to San Jose, dude."

"Right, d-u-d-e," I answer spitefully; I hate that word, I am not a dude, I'm French. Plus, why is he shouting? And why, oh why, does my Audrey live here? I can't imagine how she ended up in this place. It does not seem like her coming from the streets of London. Maybe it was not her choice, she married an American. Heaven forbid that he is anything like this taxi dude. I automatically have the feeling that I want to protect her, save her from this place, but I know I cannot.

The taxi turns into a street and stops dead. We stare incredulously at the house ahead...am I in England?

It is the most beautiful cottage, painted white with black trim with a pitched roof of wooden shingles hanging low over the windows, and surrounded by lush green lawns. It is just like a house in a fairytale, unlike any other house I have seen in America. A winding path to the door, roses, hollyhocks in bloom, it is an absolute picture.

"Some house," remarks my taxi driver, and pockets my dollars. He has a long drive home, but with a bit of luck will get fares along the way. I straighten my jacket and walk up the winding path and pull the bell cord. Clang, Clang. I am shaking like a leaf, no response. Nobody home, oh well, I will just hang around for a while.

A neighbour walks by." They are on holiday, I believe, they went to Europe."

I call back." Any idea when they are due home?"

"They just left."

"Thanks," I reply. "Lovely house isn't it?" I keep looking, still amazed by the fairytale house.

"The children round here call it The Peter Rabbit House."

I smile. That sounds like Audrey.

"Excuse me, is there anywhere I can eat round here?"

"Just turn right at the end of the street, lots of places to eat around here." He points and gestures to the right.

I walk round to the back of the house. It is so pristine, so Audrey; trust her to create this unique house. I wander around the garden and find a large crop of healthy vegetables, a variety of fruit trees, and a gazebo fitting snugly in the corner. I wander over. Inside is a white wicker couch and chairs, a table, and a chaise

Limerence

lounge with beautiful soft cushions. My Audrey has created this, her very own heavenly spot. This must be where she spends long summer afternoons reading the latest novel. I know it gets quite hot in California, what an idyllic retreat. After a busy morning gardening she must flop down in here. She reads and dozes, her husband brings tea on a tray and they discuss their next holiday. "Audrey," I whisper, " It is you who has created your own paradise. I am happy for you and sad that you are not with me."

How does this compare with my French Villa? Would she be happy there? The weather is different, quite cold in winter compared with California, but think of the culture at one's fingertips.

I leave my bag in the gazebo and wander round to the shops. There are plenty of take-away joints, this is America. People are carrying large packages and giant drink containers. No wonder that they are so fat, like the taxi driver. I select an assortment of fries, a slice of greasy pizza, take it back to the gazebo and make myself comfortable. "I might even spend the night here on your chaise lounge, Audrey darling, which might be the closest I can ever be with you." I eat supper, settle down under a heavy throw-over, lie back and compose a letter in my head for you.

Audrey Darling,

I have flown a thousand miles across a thousand seas to be with you, and you are not here, but somewhere else on Earth. We are but ships passing in the night. I have decided to spend the night in your gazebo, on your chaise to feel as close to you as I possibly can in this lifetime. Oh, how I wish I could spend just one night with you. I am so far from home, how perfect would it be if you were here with me now. I am so terribly lonely, and lost without you...

I awake to the sound of rustling; it is dawn, there is a chill in the air. A chipmunk is running up and down a tree trunk. I lie still, watching him go about his business. I think of your life here, it appears to be pretty darned good, I am happy for you, but sad for me. I wander round to the shops and sit down to a huge American breakfast. I make enquiries to find how I can get to San Francisco by train, changing a couple of times. I have all the time in the world and I take one last look at Audrey's fairytale cottage and collect my bag. The thirty-one roses are looking sad now but I leave them on the table next to the chaise. Darling Audrey, I would have liked to write you a note but I do not want to cause you trouble. You will, I am sure, suspect that someone has been here. I leave the gazebo looking slightly disturbed, leaving behind the faint linger of my presence, cigarette butts. I wonder if you will know it was me, but how possibly could you?

I blow Audrey a kiss and make my way to the train station. I find a hotel in San Francisco and spend a few days wandering around, getting to know the place. It is an interesting city but I cannot help thinking how marvellous it would be if you were showing me the sights. There is a wonderful art gallery, I spend hours there pondering art, and you. I see there is good cultural life here, concerts, plays and a symphony orchestra, and I am sure she is enjoying a full life. I visit the law courts but don't make myself known. The procedures are similar to ours, but Judge Judy is nowhere to be seen. The hills of San Francisco have tested my heart, making me short of breath, and I have to pause frequently, I feel like an old man; my medication may need adjusting.

I arrived in America with great expectations, but somehow that has evaporated. I'm not really interested in life anymore. I write the very last entry in my note book.

Los Gatos, California 1979

Audrey,

I was on your doorstep, but you were nowhere to be seen. No sunshine, it is raining in my world. Hope is over.

Hubert.

CHAPTER FIFTEEN

Hubert

I cannot smile anymore, not that I ever did much. The light in my heart has gone out, no more Audrey to be found, and my heart feels so very heavy, as though it were buried ten feet underground. Hope is a wonderful thing, if you can see where hope is hiding.

California has stolen my hope, and I have returned to France empty handed and with a broken heart; all hope is gone. I am sixty-eight years old and have been diagnosed with heart disease of which there is no cure. I am on medication which will keep the condition controlled to a certain extent, but surgery is needed. The doctors blame my heavy smoking, but I know the real reason—I'm suffering from a broken heart. I light up another Gauloises, take a long inhalation and exhale all my sadness into smoke. For a while

I tried nicotine patches, but it was all useless, and I went back to nursing my various addictions, including Audrey.

My local physician is urging me to go to Paris to see a heart surgeon, and at his insistence, and the added pressure of Juliette's pleading, I eventually cave in and make the appointment. It is soon arranged. Juliette will come to Besçanon this weekend and accompany me to Paris. Heidi has a terrible cold and would not come, even if she had been well. Why should I not be surprised? We have grown further and further apart.

Much research has been done on heart transplant surgery in recent years which gives me hope of success. In the end it happens that Lille Hospital has the necessary equipment and some very fine specialists. I must be on standby for a call any hour, so my bag is packed and by the front door day and night. Darling Audrey, if only I could discuss this with you; there is a chance of more years and maybe the possibility of meeting up with you one day. It is this that drives me on.

The hospital has done myriads of blood tests, taken so many tissue samples that I feel like a bit of raw meat, all for the match needed. I cannot have one that doesn't match, it would be fatal.

I have been preparing myself mentally for the operation and reading as much literature as possible about organ transplants. Of course it is quite possible that I won't make it; my body is pretty well gone. I will die and my secret addiction to Audrey will never be revealed.

My reading on heart transplants has revealed an unexpected possibility, one that could alter my decision. A very strange thing has been discovered about organ transplants, heart transplants in particular. It is called cellular memory, and it has been shown that memory is not confined to the brain, but may also be stored in other cells of the body, especially the heart. Proven studies show that the recipient of a new heart can take on the memories of the previous owner, and demonstrate traits of the previous owner, such as a fetish for hamburgers and coke, or poetry and champagne.

My God! What would I do if I got such a one? I would hate it. I have never been inside a McDonald's; it is disgusting, and I am not about to start now. I have my own likes and dislikes, why would I want someone else's? So, do I want a new heart? Well, yes, I want to live. It is true that I could exercise more, stop smoking, could walk and do more for my heart, fix my diet, but – my heart is filled with only Audrey.

I light up another cigarette, draw, inhale and exhale. I try to suppress a deep cough, but cannot—and the dark stabbing pain that comes as a result makes me think of my heart, imagining my four chambers filling with nicotine, and my poisoned blood flowing forth, carrying all types of toxins to my brain.

I imagine a chamber orchestra locked inside there trying to play sweet music, but suffocating in all the smoke-filled rooms. Violinists bang desperately on all four walls, trapped in ventricular linings trying to get out. Bach's Air on a G string becomes a bloodied, hideous arrangement; a jumbled, tragic mess of bittersweet notes, and one lonely violin struggles on in a pleading, whining tone, in what is left of my poor, weakened heartstrings. The horn blows to signal the alarm, the tuba booms, and the violins cry and howl at the moon as I crescendo to my final climax.

A timpanist marks my moment of death as the cymbals clash and echo tinnily throughout the land, then fade to nothing as the lights go out. I am the conductor of my own symphonic demise, and I wave my baton about like a madman. I hold my head in my hands like Tchaikovsky until the music stops and my head falls off.

Curtains, I cough and cough, the violent nicotine is having its way with me.

My colleagues have been alerted to my impending operation; I could be called at any time, and they must be in a position to take over. They are all very good, though none as much as myself; one is a former student of mine who will continue lecturing at the university in my stead; another is destined for Paris, and that is pleasing.

Propped up on pillows, drowsy and sad, it comes to me, a bolt of lightning striking my brain, 'Cellular Memory.' My heart holds the memory of Audrey, of every moment I spent with her, every thought, every longing. If I had a heart transplant I would lose all of that! There would be some stupid gibberish instead. No! I will not have it replaced at any cost. I could not. I would sooner die than give up the memories of my Audrey.

I want to leap out of bed and phone Juliette. My limbs are galvanised, my heart singing. Heidi comes the following day keeping to her routine of looking after me; she is such a good woman. She takes the news calmly, says she understands, she's obviously resigned to whatever whims affect me.

I phone Juliette, who is disappointed, but heartened by my pledge to cut out cigarettes and fatty food. The two women in my life may be curious as to why I have made this decision, but it is for them to wonder, and for me to know. The third one, Audrey, already knows. I will leave my life in God's hands, it is his will from here on. Meanwhile, I continue to live out my daydreams for the rest of my days with my darling English rose.

CHAPTER SIXTEEN

Juliette

I make my regular call to Papa on Saturday morning. He doesn't answer, so I think he is probably in the garden. I try an hour later, but still no answer. I'm about to call my mother, but the phone rings out instead. Thinking it will be Papa, I start to say something bright, but it's Mother. She is weeping, sobbing, distraught.

"He's dead." These two words bring total despair to my heart. I have loved him all my life, he has been so kind, helpful, guiding me to follow his path into the law, and goading me into finding my life experiences.

"How?" Tears stream down my face.

Limerence

"I found him crumpled in a heap in his office, slumped over his desk this morning. He was clutching a photograph, and a little note book. Oh, my dear—come quickly, please."

I rush to the train station and arrive to find Mama a complete mess. We dissolve into each other's arms. Her friends arrive, who overwhelm us with their talk of food, flowers and sympathy. His old school friend, Jacques, comes out of the blue, such a nice man, and tells us stories about their early life as teens together.

Time goes by unheeded; the next thing I remember is the autopsy, which determines that Papa had suffered a massive heart attack. Then the funeral; all those dignitaries and praise, the university giving his name to the faculty. How great a man he was. How hard it will be to live up to his example. Then the walk back with Mama. The desk, the book, the letters – oh, all those things.

I had been surprised to see how devastated Mama had been; they had seemed so detached, led different lives, lived in different houses and had different tastes. "He was my reason for living, we marked time together," she tells me, which seems rather strange.

I ask how they met, but she turns red and stutters – maybe it had been a quick fling in her village, having to get married, the stillbirth. I don't care. It must have been awful to be in Germany after the war; it was her chance to get away.

Well, it's all over now. I sit once more at his desk, where as a girl I had dreamed of sitting, but was never allowed. I look at all his books, at his pictures, his old gramophone. He was cultured, refined, and I can only hope I will be the same, to honour his memory.

Mama comes in and hands me a black and white photo. "This is the picture he had in his hand when he died," she tells me, "and this is the note book, a list of all his desires, the dates he wrote about her. Look here, he writes, "Oh, she ruined my life—no, she changed it forever; it was mine to ruin, no matter what."

The girl was indeed pretty, I suppose about nineteen; she had such an open face, full lips, gorgeous smile, mass of curly blonde hair. The picture looks old fashioned now, but she'd caught his heart at the time and never let it go.

I look up now at this woman in my presence, my mother of thirty five years, and I see the strength, the sadness, the incredible love she has for me.

"Look, Mama," I say, smiling, "You have never told me how you managed to marry Papa. I began to think you must have got pregnant, just so you could get out of Germany. But, look—I know you very well, and that cannot be true. It isn't, is it? Tell me the truth." Mama is grinning, a big wide grin.

"Oh no, my love. I just asked him to marry me. And he said 'Yes.'

CHAPTER SEVENTEEN

Heidi

What a strange marriage I have had. Years living a loveless life, being overwhelmed by bitterness at Hubert's lack of affection, indifference to passion and sex. If it hadn't been for my German strength of will and the determination to not give in, I would not have survived. Not being able to conceive for so long, and blaming myself for his disappointments; trying all manner of things to appease him, to no avail, all the time without the slightest hint of comfort or sympathy.

To see him drift off into his infatuation with that stupid English woman—for years it made me want to scream. Even one real kiss, one arm around my waist would have been something—but no, his heart, it was a refrigerator, an icebox of impassivity that broke my heart. Even when I lost my temper and struck him one time there was no reaction, just, 'I'll go make the coffee. 'There were the occasional breadcrumbs of recognition of course, which was almost enough to forgive him, for he was a great man in every other respect.

I would have left him though, if it had not been for my daughter, the miracle that brought beams of sunshine to my life. This was my life's yearning; my whole desire in life was to have a child, and through the birth of Juliette I began to live, rather than just exist.

But, as I look back now, I see it hasn't all been bad. Who would have thought that when I came across that lone French soldier on guard in our village that he would turn out to be so famous. I was amazed at all the accolades he was given. He really was a brilliant lawyer and judge, and the respect I was given by everyone at the funeral was uplifting and gratifying, even the mayor's wife was friendly. My German origins were, in reality, nothing; same for my lack of education, which in the past had made me withdraw from his friends because their scholarly ways made me feel so inferior. I was truly French to them, a worthy wife to such a man. I will live here now in peace and happiness.

Juliette comes to stand by my side. She is truly devastated by the loss of her father. I put my arm around her waist, lean over and kiss her cheek.

"You are beautiful," I tell her, "strong and practical like me, very clever and dedicated like your father, and it is wonderful to know we both brought you up to be honest and trustworthy. I love you so much."

She looks at me, tears in her eyes.

"Mama, I have – had, well I still do, in a way—the best parents anyone could wish for. Thank you." She hugs me, then adds, "I don't think I've ever said that to you before."

I look at my daughter then, she is the height of French fashion; she looks so chic, looking as though she just walked out of a fashion house. Hubert had been mighty proud of how his French-German daughter had turned out, and was never shy at saying so. "Look at my girl," he'd say. "Isn't she beautiful?"

I am so proud of Juliette. Her academic ability, her skill, her confidence in everything she chooses to do. Three years ago she obtained her pilot's license. Hubert had bought her a little piper two-seater as a reward for obtaining her articles, and went with her on her first solo flight; I was too scared at the time, but Hubert was bursting with pride. Now she will carry on his legacy, the Law, the Academy.

The following day the practicalities of the future weigh on my mind. Not the will, the legal things, but the house, the living. Mon Dieu! I am a widow. No more responsibilities to my husband but free to do what I want. I have my own beautiful villa, and money is no problem, and my sisters can visit, and I can travel, and see all those places I have only ever seen on television.

But first things first. Juliette will not return to her law firm until the following day, but what will become of this enormous house, the 'Chateau 'as the locals call it; will she continue to hang onto it? It has been left to her by her father and is worth a fortune. She might want to sell it.

I call her and ask what she wants to do. I have never been one for subtlety, but she's used to that, and says without hesitation that she has thought this through.

" Of course I'll keep it. I will live here. It's my home, it has always been home. We'll have parties, all my friends will come, and you—you'll come, Mama, won't you? As often as you like, though I know you have never really liked it. You used to call it 'the grand French pile of stone,' do you remember? But it's yours too, so you are welcome—more than that, just come."

I feel a rush of happiness. My daughter is so warm, so loving. "Good. I'll be there tomorrow to start cleaning. You know me, I cook, I clean. It is my expertise. I suppose you will be back at work, so I'll have free reign of the house, every room, every corner will gleam under my magic fingers."

She laughs. "Mama, you are incorrigible. Very well, have fun."

Limerence

CHAPTER EIGHTEEN

Juliette

I muse over Mama's words. She is so practical, so down to earth, I am just like her and can feel her German-ness in my bones. She has taught me the power of fortitude, her loyalty and ability to honour her pledges, so much more than the people of today. She looks at things with clear eyes, and works out what the future could be, and goes after it without hesitation. In hindsight, she is quite the opposite to Papa, who approached things in a most careful and deliberate, controlled manner. Yet such sadness exists for my mother, for having a husband who did not love her. Who loved A— oh my, I suddenly remember those letters, those aerograms in my father's desk, that secret drawer, that little book.

I cannot let her find these letters. Her life has been sad enough. If she ever found them it would be too much. She may be stoic, but she is still flesh and blood. I run up the stairs and stop, overcome by the books, the papers spread across the desk, the odour of his cigarettes. Tears come unbidden. My father. My hero, my idol, a genius with a secret that hurt no one but him. I go to the window and look at this beautiful town; I see the river, the citadel, and I can feel its history and the way it has been a backdrop to my life. And his. I sit at his desk, put my head on my arms and weep.

Five minutes later and I'm pulling that drawer open, taking out those letters, the small notebook kept hidden, and I can sense my father's impossible dream. It was what it was, and I can do nothing about it, but I can try to carry out his wishes. I love him through all of it, and even now it makes no difference either way. He was a man, just a man, who lived his life unfulfilled, hanging onto an unrequited love.

The pink ribbon has come loose, so I straighten and smooth the envelopes before carefully re-tying it. Such clear, cursive script she had. She must have been beautiful; she must have had some quality that mesmerised him, that he could never let go. I feel a pang of pity, sense some of his misery. I pick up the little notebook and once more I force myself to read the writing on the cover.

'If ever I should die, send this book to Audrey. She has been my grand adventure from which I am still suffering. She has been my only friend, and will keep forever my devotion.'

I open the book and look at some of the entries. Every one has the same date in April, starting in 1949. I turn the pages at random.

'The sun is shining as it was thirty eight years ago. Every day I am with you.'

Another page, this time short.

The sun is here, but what next?'

On the third page;

'I am in my office, suddenly I feel I have to look at your photo. The sun is shining wherever you are. I would like to dial your number but I am too shy. Perhaps one day before I leave this world.'

The last page is smeared, probably with his tears.

'Thursday. No sunshine. It's raining. Hope is over.'

I put the book and the letters in a small box and take it downstairs to my bedroom and place it carefully in my briefcase. I will honour my father's last, dying request and send on the letters and notebook to this woman named Audrey. I'm so very curious. I would like to meet this woman who so occupied my father's life— and for his whole life. She must be something extraordinary.

CHAPTER NINETEEN

Audrey

I have just enjoyed a few days holidaying in Switzerland. I visit every couple of years to spend time with my three children. My marriage ended after twenty years—I suppose I was never cut out to be a Swiss wife. We were young when we married, it was not long after the war, and my beau wooed me with lace blouses, chocolates, all the things that we had never seen during the war. He poured his heart out to me daily with letters, and I holidayed with his family; they were so loving towards me, and I suppose I was swept off my feet. It was a fairytale wedding in an ancient church at the side of a lake. I was schooled in the ways of a Swiss wife: cooking, housekeeping, learning Swiss-German language skills, and how to keep my husband happy. We had two children quickly and then another, when I had help with a maid.

We lived in an apartment at first, but then in a lovely house that I enjoyed decorating with the antiques I bought back from my trips back to England. He gave me a French garden for Christmas, I loved it. I suppose I just wasn't cut out for the disciplined life of Switzerland, though, where business was discussed from morning to night and everything had to be just so. In the end the divorce was quite amicable; my daughter came to England with me, and the boys remained in Switzerland with their father to take on the family business. He married again, happily for everyone. His new wife was Swiss and fitted into their lifestyle beautifully, making a much loved wife and step-mother to my boys.

I went back to England and lived in the south for a while with my daughter, who attended a convent school. She is bi-lingual which has served her well through life. I had some interesting jobs in London, and we spent weekends immersed in the culture of the city. I missed the boys dreadfully, but it wasn't long before I met an American, a nuclear scientist who swept me off my feet. He was tall, handsome, witty, clever and going through a divorce like me.

Chris soon convinced me that sunny California was preferable to the inclement English weather, and to forgo my alimony and move out west with him. My father was disappointed that a 'Yank ' was luring his daughter halfway around the world. He was a successful businessman as well as a Methodist lay preacher, and I was astounded when he suggested that I live over there for three months with him, to see how the land lay between us before committing myself.

I boarded a plane, landing in San Francisco, and was met by my prince, whom I had known less than six months. Driving to his home in San Jose I mentioned my father's advice. Chris stopped the car.

"Audrey, the wedding is scheduled for next Wednesday at three o'clock. If you're having second thoughts we can turn back right now. Otherwise we will continue."

This was my new husband-to-be. Self-assured, an A1 American guy. The wedding naturally took place as scheduled, in beautiful gardens in the Californian summer. My daughter and his three daughters and son were present as well as some of his friends.

I wore a knee-length, flowing white gown with a white picture hat. I smiled and hoped for the best. It was a perfect wedding, although the first couple of years were tricky. He had children to put through college and money was tight. My daughter had trouble settling into a co-educational American High school, especially after the strict discipline of an English all-girls convent.

I hated the American drawl and missed England and my friends, but I soon got a job teaching English Literature and the History of Art in a private girl's school, which I loved; since my retirement, several ex-pupils have been in touch to thank me for what I taught them about art and literature. My new husband has a very adventurous spirit, and we bought a camper van. Every weekend we would take off to the Redwood forests, or the sunny beaches of California, and I grew to appreciate the country. I have always been an active member of the Methodist church so I soon made friends there. My husband was not interested in religion, except when food was being served, but he was accepting of me being a regular churchgoer. We lived in a nondescript street in Los Gatos in a nondescript house, but across the road was this incredibly delightful house, so different from the rest. A black and white cottage with a pitched roof, built a hundred years ago by a prominent architect. I fell in love with that house, it was so English; I used to gaze on it from my bedroom. The old lady who lived there for years died and the house auctioned. Eventually it became ours, with a life-long commitment to make it the most delightful house and garden in the district.

One day the doorbell rang and a little boy asked, "Does Peter Rabbit live here?" That is how enchanting this place truly is. My husband Chris and I worked tirelessly on the house; it has a mezzanine floor like a minstrel's gallery and all my Anglo-memorabilia looks perfect in it. While in Switzerland I had learnt to paint China; today, my friends love to come to tea in my drawing room and drink from my decorated fine porcelain cups. We gather in the Gazebo in the summer; I lie on my chaise in the hot summer afternoons and read our latest book club suggestions.

The children finally finished school, and my daughter chose to go back to Switzerland; she missed her brothers and her Father. Chris's children took up various careers; one a lawyer, another an airline pilot, another in hospital administration. They all have very successful, fruitful lives.

Meanwhile I have to think about this strange occurrence in my life, a bundle of letters returned to me in the post, ones that I wrote to a French boy I met when I was nineteen—and whom I have completely forgotten about. The accompanying letter is from his daughter; it tells me he has died and that she, Juliette, is anxious to meet me. My husband Chris is not so amused.

"What are you worried about, Chris!" I exclaim. "The man is dead!" Chris returns my gaze with the most deadpan expression and sighs.

"Dead men are the worst."

CHAPTER TWENTY

Audrey

Juliette has offered to pick me up in her plane, but never having met her, I think it advisable to go by train to Besçanon, which is not far from the Swiss border. I am rather concerned as to what she will think of me, an old lady of seventy-three, though I am in good shape, exercise daily, and watch my carbs, so I should not be concerned.

I arrive at the station on a beautiful summer's day, alight from the train, turn to walk up the platform when a gorgeous young woman approaches me with outstretched arms. She is wearing a yellow dress dotted with white flowers and her dark hair is fashioned in a smart French chignon; her skin glows with a lovely summer tan. She is stunning. My mind is trying to recall the Frenchman with the long nose and similar dark hair, but her eyes are a charcoal blue. I catch glimpses of her shapely figure through the sheer dress shimmering in the sun. Everything about her screams impeccable, from her silver earrings and glittery jewels on her fingers. She is like my own daughter who is in Switzerland.

"You must be Audrey." She holds out her shapely hand, "I am so happy to meet you. I am Juliette, Hubert's daughter. I have been longing to meet you ever since my father died and I discovered your letters." We embrace warmly, and she takes my arm. We jump into her little sport's car and drive over the cobbled streets of Besçanon.

She chats as we drive along, pointing out the Gallo-Roman remains and 18th Century facades of the Place de Revolution. It is a beautiful town, a small city, and she gives me a summary of its history, all in perfect English.

"My father impressed upon me the importance of speaking languages and developing the art of conversation."

"You do that very well indeed." She is vivacious, supremely confident, but it is still hard for me to recall her father. We continue to chat and I feel that I have known her for a long time.

I try to imagine Hubert as a young lawyer walking the streets, his face serious, briefcase in hand. He must have been very clever and cultured.

The car stops, and we pull up outside a stunning French villa. It's not unlike Monet's house, painted pink with green shutters, and I feel a pang of jealousy. Juliette helps me with my bag, and we walk up the garden path that leads to a huge oak door; I look past the door and see a long passage with rooms on either side. We walk down the hall; it is breathtaking, each room is filled with the most exquisite antique furniture, fit for a museum. Books line the walls, classical music plays softly in the background and musical notes dance around the red Toile De Jouy wallpapered rooms.

"How my father would have loved to show you this house. In a way he created it for you."

'Oh dear,' I think, but instead say, "Where is your mother?"

"Oh Audrey, she hates this house and its antiques. Many years ago, Papa bought another house for her in town, much more to her taste; it is near the market and the park where she can walk her little dog. To be honest, my parents should never have married, they had nothing in common."

I sigh and nod quietly. What can I say? We walk through the kitchen to the verandah, which overlooks a charming French garden. We rest in white wicker furniture, sip tea and feast on Madeleines. Juliette asks me about my life in California and extols the virtues of her father.

"He was my hero, he reached the very top of his profession and was truly admired by all."

I have to be impressed, yet a feeling of sadness accompanies my mixed emotions. He had apparently dwelt on me all is life to no avail. I cannot help thinking of the irony of life, and the invisible scars that we leave on one another that we are completely unaware of.

Juliette suggests a visit to his grave, so I pick a white rose and we walk to the cemetery. The grave is an impressive marble slab with gold lettering. Juliette translates the wording on the epitaph for me, lists her Father's achievements and honours. I place the rose on the grave and utter a silent prayer. I thank him for his utter devotion and apologise for all the distress I unknowingly caused.

As we walk back to the house Juliette tells me what her Mother said on the day of the funeral.

"I was married to a man who was in love with another woman all my married life."

I feel mortified for that poor woman. I can remember what it was like to be in a loveless marriage during the later years of my Swiss marriage. It was agony to wake up every day to this cold, detached human being. I want to meet her mother to apologise, but I am sure she would not be pleased. I never do meet her.

Juliette says, "Audrey, without a shadow of a doubt, my father thought very highly of you, he was in love with you. Since meeting you, I can understand why."

"The tragedy was that he never knew me, and also I never really knew him. The fact is, this relationship was a *limerent* affair, my dear. I was his unwitting *limerent* lover and never knew."

"Limerence? What is that?"

"Well, it is something called Limerence, where there is no actualisation of love; it's a fixation on the unobtainable. It is..."—I put my hand on her arm, hoping this beautiful young woman will not be upset by my next words—" an aberration, a rare mental condition. He was able to sustain and continue such levels of infatuation because it is unattainable, it never was. I have been a doing a little research of my own, and it appears your father would fit the criteria for love addiction. It is something akin to a functioning alcoholic; they become addicted to the feeling of euphoria, the dream-like aspect of a love that does not bear fruit, but subsists solely on infatuation, feeding off its own dream-like interpretation. I think if our love had come to fruition, I can almost guarantee that it would never have been able to sustain itself. His infatuation with me I now think resulted in him creating something called the halo effect, where I became the perfect creature in his mind and could do no wrong. Can you see that?"

I look at Juliette's face, she looked crestfallen. I know she wants to believe in the truth of it all, and my harsh words about her father's infatuation cut sharply. I reach out for her hand, and smile. Her chignon is unravelling, wisps are falling out gently over her face, and her sad eyes look back at me, not wanting to believe the truth about her father's romantic fantasy, this stuff of Romeo and Juliet. We both take a moment to observe a visiting sparrow peck at scattered madeleine crumbs.

"But... my father was an intelligent man, a Judge no less, professor and Dean of Law. He was serious, steady, highly respected. Yet, judging from all those letters he wrote, his diary, he was totally in love with you." She looks baffled, sad and confused.

"Just listen to today's rock music," I say." It's all about love being pain and suffering, the extremes of euphoria—but this is simply not true. Real love is imperfect, real love is messy, real love is unkind sometimes, and real love is seeing the flaws in the other and still loving them. Real love is not crazy or obsessive or lustful; it is slow, patient, kind, forgiving. I love that passage in Shakespeare, do you know the one?

> *Love is not love that alters when*
> *it alteration finds, nor bends with the*
> *remover to remove,*
> *Oh no, it is an ever fix'ed mark,*
> *that looks on tempests*
> *and is never shaken.*

Limerence

Juliette's eyes well with tears and she squeezes my hand tightly.

"Darling Juliette. I am afraid that I am upsetting you. This must be heartbreaking for you. Your father wore his heart on his sleeve. I am a more pragmatic person than he; I tend to lean more towards logic than emotion. I just don't get carried away in the moment, which is why I never saw my days with your father as anything more than a lovely week of fun and flirtation. Clearly, your father saw it very differently; but one week is a thin basis for such lasting emotion. I think Hubert had a very hyper-idealised idea of me, which is just not true. He thought I was something extraordinary, but I am not. I am quite forgettable, which I do remember telling him, all those years ago. I am so sorry for all the pain I caused him—and you—but it was entirely innocent."

Juliette shakes her head and insists I have done nothing wrong. She tells me that her mother does not know of my visit and is in fact visiting her family in Germany. This is a relief to me as I don't want to come face to face with a woman who will probably want to knife me.

"My sweet Juliette, you are a smart, beautiful woman, I find it hard to believe that you have not married."

"Oh Audrey, I have dreamed of meeting a man, but it seems an impossibility because I am looking for someone like my father. It is truly awful, and this town is very small, and Paris so busy, the men so – ugly." She almost spits the word out.

I want to tell Juliette not to spend her whole life looking for the impossible dream the way her father had, but the cruelty of the words sting sharply on my own tongue. We have talked ourselves to exhaustion and I am feeling tired.

We go back to the grand house. We have supper, and Juliette shows me to my room, makes me comfortable and tells me that this was his bedroom, his bed. As I slide between the crisp linen sheets I can't help feeling strange. I look around the room which has a very masculine flavour with its sturdy mahogany bed and tallboy. One of those chairs with something to hold a man's suit, a valet stand I think they call it, a chest of drawers with brass handles, and an enormous antique wardrobe with elaborate, carved scrolls. Two nice watercolours of the French countryside sit upon the walls, and a Tiffany lamp sits by the bedside. I search for his taste in his books, his objets d'art. There is a large photograph of him in judicial robe atop the bureau looking quite the distinguished gentleman. Strong nose, unlined kindly face, his dark hair now grey. I never knew this man, though I am slowly getting to know him, ironically in death more than in life. His musical tastes, the bound volumes that line the book shelves, all alphabetised, the faint smell of cigarette smoke in the finely woven Aubusson rug.

There is also a photograph of a younger man, and I do remember his features. He is wearing shorts and a shirt and carrying a tennis racquet. Quite handsome, I think, and it serves to alert my old memory. I look out through the quaint French windows to the mountains beyond which they call the seven hill-tops, as seven mountains protect the village like the walls of its heart.

Juliette has made little mention of her mother, and I wonder about this woman who married him. Did she tolerate his obsession with me, his secrecy? I feel a strong sense of admiration for her—I don't think I could stay married to a man whose heart belonged to somebody else. Had I been her, I suspect that I would have left Hubert years ago; what some women will tolerate in the name of love is unfathomable to me. I sleep fitfully, and wake in the night

Limerence

with the distinct feeling that someone is in the room. I call out, "Juliette, is that you?" but there is no reply beyond the dark, still night. Could it be the ghost of Hubert? I lie there thinking: why on earth was Hubert so taken with me? It does not sit well in my mind. If only he had realised that there was nothing exceptional about me, that I tread this earth, a flawed individual like everyone else.

It then occurs to me that I am hurting my own marriage by being here. I wonder how Chris is coping, I must ring him tomorrow.

The next day Juliette asks me if I would like to see Besçanon from the air. I think, why not, she seems such a competent young lady. I strap myself into this cute little plane and she proudly tells me it was a present from her father when she completed her exams.

We back out of the hanger on a perfect blue sky day, sunshine and very little wind. What beautiful countryside it is when viewed from the air. It seems a privilege to swoop over this lovely place nestled by the side of the Doube river, as it meanders through roaming countryside. The majestic Jura Mountains provided a natural barrier during the many wars it has taken part in, from the Middle Ages to Julius Caesar to World War II, when the Germans executed one hundred French Resistance fighters in the Citadel. Juliette gives me a running commentary of the history and all the historical buildings. It is fascinating.

Another night in Hubert's bed, and I experience nothing, except—now, what did I just hear? Was that a faint distant cough? 'Too many cigarettes, Hubert? 'I think. That would have been hard for me to tolerate too. I had quite a battle with Chris trying to quit, which ended with my threatening to leave. And I did, for three days. He begged me to come back. I did, and we have had a smoke free life ever since—and as far as I am aware.

The next day we stop for croissants and coffee, then Juliette drives me to the airport. It is a strange farewell, almost like family, but not. Juliette is quite emotional and I cannot help wondering what lasting effect her father's idiosyncrasies have had on his daughter, possibly leaving a distorted view of relationships, or of love, for that matter. She hands me a box containing the bundle of letters tied in pink ribbon, and tells me that they are mine now, they belong to me. She bids me 'à bientôt,' which she says is the French custom and promise 'to meet again;' for the French never say 'au revoir' or goodbye to true friendship.

I leave for the States, and when the plane lands I fall into the arms of my darling husband. If anything, this trip has been edifying in terms of my marriage; Chris hugs me tight as if reclaiming me, and I feel safe and back home where I belong.

Chris is a most handsome creature; he is so tall and dependable. It must be the Nordic Viking in him that attracted me so long ago. His hair is greying now, and thinning a little, but he has a long, distinguished nose and a great sense of humour; he truly knows how to make me laugh. He hugs me tight, as if re- claiming me, and it is quite surreal, my tall, dependable, husband.

Brought up as an only child on the rough streets of Chicago, his father was a postal worker and knew the name of every street in Chicago. Chris was bright at school, worked his way through college and university to become a nuclear physicist. His job has taken him all over the world. He is a deep thinker, a man of few words and many ideas. When I first met him, he was carrying a copy of Ted Hughes 'poetry under his arm.

" Well I never!" I said." Ted holidayed at my house in Switzerland when he was dating my sister. They met in Cambridge, and one time he actually painted a lion on my dining room wall!" That was always a great conversation starter.

We arrive at our Peter Rabbit House, and my first job is to inspect the garden. The roses need dead heading, and some fruit is ready for picking; I have missed my garden as much as I have missed Chris. The grass is neatly cut, a job Chris prides himself upon. I have mooted fake grass, but he is appalled at the thought; maybe one day when he is no longer up to the task. The vegetable garden looks supreme, we are going to have a good crop of tomatoes for sauce this year; the fruit trees are loaded with apricots, peaches, and persimmon. I will be very busy preparing them for freezing for my daily smoothie. Chris likes to do the shopping to choose the right cut of meat to barbecue. I have a charmed life, exercises in the morning where we learn dances to perform at nursing homes, as well as events in the park. We call ourselves 'The sizzling Seniors, 'where many are over eighty some are in their nineties. We wear outrageous costumes; California is full of ageing dancers who hit the stage back in their early life. I garden in the morning, recline with a book in my gazebo in the afternoon and prepare dinner in the evening. Chris organises all our travels, I just pack my bag and go along with his ideas. Sometimes it might be staying in youth hostels, or five-star hotels. Whatever; life with Chris is an adventure. The only thing that bugs me is his watching sport on T.V. probably because I am English and don't know a thing about American football. He was a champion tennis player in college so we enjoy watching that together. We subscribe to the plays and symphony concerts in San Francisco; I can't imagine I could have had a better life in France. Who knows, Chris is baffled by the whole French scenario, his practical mind just cannot envisage it.

I write to Juliette.

Los Gatos, 2008

My Dear Juliette,

It is with great fondness that I remember our wonderful time together in Besçanon. We became united through sad circumstances over the loss of your wonderful father, and I treasure our new-found friendship and the special time we shared. Since I returned home Chris is planning our next holiday; I hope that he will have the privilege of meeting you one day. I am sure you are busy with your Law Practice and keeping up your beautiful house in your father's memory. I can imagine you sitting at your father's desk doing important work, or taking a stroll on the old cobbled Rues to buy your daily baguette and cheese.

I must tell you about the wonderful book I am reading on the history of Besçanon; it is a most interesting read. Chris is an avid reader and likes to read history. The last time we spoke it was about your father's love for me, but I have been reflecting upon this and have to tell you that his first real love was for you, not me – that was just a fantasy - it was you of course, his daughter who had his heart.

Please forgive my ramblings, although I feel I can tell you my thoughts because of the friendship we have formed. I hope my revelations bring you comfort my dear Juliette, and I do hope life continues to treat you well.

Fondly,

Audrey.

A week later I am surprised and thrilled to receive a letter from Juliette. I hurriedly make myself a pot of tea and sit down in the garden to savour it.

Besçanon, 2008

Dear Audrey,
How wonderful and joyous it was to receive your letter! It is lovely to hear that your return travels were safe and you have settled back into your beautiful Californian life. I so enjoyed your visit to Besçanon, and to finally meet the woman my father adored. You are every bit as wonderful as I had hoped. I have been enjoying more holidays, and in September went to the forest where I saw and heard the bells on the stags. In October I visited Pantan in Brazil where I met many jaguars and lots of coloured birds. At home again, I like to observe birds in my garden, it brings me such peace, I am at one with nature. I am always interested to hear about your time with my father. Please keep in touch and write me from time to time. I so enjoy your company and do feel we will be kindred spirits forever.

Fondly,
Juliette.

I place the letter on the table and smile to myself. What a beautiful new friendship that has blossomed between myself and this young girl. I go in search of Chris to tell him of the letter. He would normally be in his office behind his computer where he likes playing the stock market, or planning our next holiday. Today he is fiddling with his beloved camera. He is the consummate American tourist with his camera always at the ready, and we have amassed thousands of slides, looking at them occasionally and reminiscing.

A perfect sunset builds on the horizon, turning the foothills of Saratoga to smooth indigo silhouettes; twinkling stars come out to greet us under the vast Californian sky. I watch as Chris tinkers with the lens, adjusting it to zoom in upon an unwitting object of his desire. A popping pansy or ant carrying his evening load of crumbs back to his entire village.

"How are you feeling, sweetheart? Still tired from your long journey?" Chris asks.

"Well, I just received a lovely letter from Juliette. Besçanon is a beautiful town, it is known as the secret city. I think Hubert must have liked that; from what I gather he was a bit aloof—intelligent, but a strange old man. Juliette gave me a guided tour. Oh, I tasted the most exquisite pastries and desserts. Chris, you should have seen the patisseries. I indulged myself in the decadence of French life. They certainly know how to live well over there. But it is not my life. She is the most darling girl, Chris, a beautiful French girl. I hope you will meet her one day. She may come to California."

"I'm sure I will one day, dear. I forgot to tell you, but the kids will be over at the weekend, they missed you too."

We do not need to speak more about Hubert. I have been through the strangest experience. It seems quite surreal now, for both of us; it is beyond belief to discover that a man has been in love with me for his whole life, to the detriment of himself and his family. I hope I met with Juliette's expectations. I think often of Heidi, how that poor woman endured a loveless marriage, and all because of me—while I, totally oblivious, quietly got on with my life on the other side of the world. Chris is just mystified by the whole thing. It is hard to imagine what my life would have been like with Hubert. I doubt that it would have been anything as fulfilling as my marriage to Chris. I look up into his eyes expectantly and he knows I am about to say something important.

"Darling, I have been thinking about this question since I boarded the plane in Paris:

"Is it better to love, or to be loved?"

Chris looks at me thoughtfully. I can always trust my husband to take the time he needs to give me his most considered responses. Our love is consistent, long lasting. Real love is steady, like a ship that ploughs through turbulent seas, unmoved by the forces of nature, continuing on through any weather, unabated, undeterred. This is our life; this is our love.

After a minute or so he says, "Well, I think it's better to love than be loved, because the very act of loving in itself, is pleasurable. It brings feelings of euphoria to the self. But it is a selfish act when one stops and truly thinks about it, isn't it? And this word, love, it is ambiguous, no? We cannot do anything about *who* it is that loves us, for in this situation we are really only the recipient of that kind of love, which is a love beyond control. Right?"

He puts down his camera, and grabs me by the waist.

"Let's not go on with this needless folly, we can feel it in each other's lovely old bones. What a glorious life we share together, I never want it to end." He wraps me in his arms.

"The correct answer to your question is that it is reciprocal love that is the best love. That which is given and received without hindrance." Chris holds me tight and whispers in my ear. "I love you, Audrey."

Limerence

CHAPTER TWENTY-ONE

Audrey

San Jose, May 2018

Dear Hubert,

Today is your birthday and I feel impelled to write to you. What a lot has happened since you died in 1993. You would be eighty-eight today. I remember that when we met in 1948 you told me of your fear of communism sweeping over France. It didn't happen of course; communism has crumbled and capitalism has taken over in Russia. The last time Chris and I were over there we asked for more pancakes for breakfast, but only if we paid another two dollars. Of course we refused.

Incidentally, I get on very well with your daughter Juliette who is a knockout, and still unmarried at thirty-five. One day I said to her, "How come a beautiful girl like you is not married?" She replied, "I am looking for someone like my father." There can never be anyone to fit that criteria. My second husband Chris died seven years ago and I miss him dreadfully. I suspect you have met him in that place far, far away. I often think of you playing tennis together. I am eighty-nine now; how I wish you were around to liven my days. You were right when you wrote in your letters that the tragedy of life is that when one is young, healthy and ready for anything, we're broke. And yet in old age we have the cash to undertake anything, but health constrains us. Oh, how right you were. Recently I suffered heart failure; the doctors gave me the choice of whether I wished to be revived and continue living, or not. At the time I said yes, however now I wish that I had said no. So, here I am, still jogging along.

Why are you no longer here? As you know I am living in California. How I wish I could share my life with you now, and how I wish I could be loved by you now. Hubert, I have a lovely garden, lots of roses and other flowers, vegetables galore, loads of peaches and apricots. Do you remember buying peaches from the barrow boy in London? We both had peach juice running down our faces, and afterwards we went to see, 'Annie Get Your Gun.' What joy. Nowadays the music is loud and disharmonious and not much fun to sing to. How different to the sounds of our youth. I miss them dreadfully, just as I miss you.

Yours Ever,
Audrey.

Limerence

ACKNOWLEDGEMENTS

I wish to extend my deepest gratitude first and foremost to my sister Audrey for allowing me the rights to the re-telling of this incredible true story, without which this book would not be possible.

My sister has entrusted me to relay the events of this time with as much accuracy and detail as can be afforded through unlimited access to private letters and critical photographic material as evidence to support its' chronological sequence. Certain parts of this story have been fictionalised in the interest of the development of story; however, where possible we felt it our duty to remain as accurate and as close to the truth as humanly possible. Naturally, names have been changed to protect those involved. I also want to thank my co-writer, Susan Wakefield, for her tireless dedication to writing this story based on true events, and also without whom this *body of work would not be possible. Susan and I laboriously pieced together the events of the period through combined research efforts, dedicated as we were to reconstructing the story itself to pay homage to its lasting historical integrity.*

I also wish to thank my second editor, Lindsay Coker, and Agnes Gokel for sharing her experiences growing up in Germany during the war.

Lastly, I wish to thank my friends and family for their support and belief in this special project which has been close to my heart for a long time. To see it come to fruition has been my long time dream.

Sincerely,

Liz Hicklin

ABOUT THE AUTHOR

Liz Hiklin was born and educated in the U.K. The daughter of a lay preacher, Liz grew up listening to her father tell stories and was encouraged from an early age to entertain guests with poems and prose. In retirement Liz has found time to write and wax lyrical as an active member of the Peninsula Writer's Club and feature performance poet at Poet's Corner. Liz has published two books of poetry and short stories. This is her debut novel.

Susan Wakefield lived in the U.S. for twenty years as an expatriate Australian freelance writer, poet and novelist. Through Peninsula Writers, Liz and Susan have formed a formidable duo to bring to life the unforgettable true story of Limerence.

This beautiful photo was taken of Audrey in 1948 when she first met Hubert at the London Olympic Games.

This delightful building is the actual Peter Rabbit House
mentioned in the story where
Audrey Lived in California.

www.ingramcontent.com/pod-product-compliance
Lightning Source LLC
Chambersburg PA
CBHW030259010526
44107CB00053B/1759